DATE DUE

Bloom's BioCritiques

Bloom's BioCritiques

WILLIAM WORDSWORTH

Edited and with an introduction by
Harold Bloom
Sterling Professor of the Humanities
Yale University

CHELSEA HOUSE
PUBLISHERS
A Haights Cross Communications Company

Philadelphia

©2003 by Chelsea House Publishers, a subsidiary of
Haights Cross Communications.

A Haights Cross Communications Company

Introduction © 2003 by Harold Bloom.

Printed and bound in the United States of America.

10 9 8 7 6 5 4 3 2 1

Library of Congress Cataloging-in-Publication Data

William Wordsworth / edited and with an introduction by Harold Bloom.
        p. cm. -- (Bloom's biocritiques)
Includes bibliographical references and index.
  ISBN: 0-7910-7385-8
 1. Wordsworth, William, 1770–1850--Criticism and interpretation. I.
Bloom, Harold. II. Series.
  PR5888.W45 2003
  821'.7--dc21

                                                    2003006920

Chelsea House Publishers
1974 Sproul Road, Suite 400
Broomall, PA 19008-0914

http://www.chelseahouse.com

Contributing editor: Neil Heims

Cover design by Keith Trego

Cover: © Bettman/CORBIS

Layout by EJB Publishing Services

CONTENTS

User's Guide

These volumes are designed to introduce the reader to the life and work of the world's literary masters. Each volume begins with Harold Bloom's essay "The Work in the Writer" and a volume-specific introduction also written by Professor Bloom. Following these unique introductions is an engaging biography that discusses the major life events and important literary accomplishments of the author under consideration.

Furthermore, each volume includes an original critique that not only traces the themes, symbols, and ideas apparent in the author's works, but strives to put those works into a cultural and historical perspective. In addition to the original critique is a brief selection of significant critical essays previously published on the author and his or her works followed by a concise and informative chronology of the writer's life. Finally, each volume concludes with a bibliography of the writer's works, a list of additional readings, and an index of important themes and ideas.

HAROLD BLOOM

The Work in the Writer

Literary biography found its masterpiece in James Boswell's *Life of Samuel Johnson*. Boswell, when he treated Johnson's writings, implicitly commented upon Johnson as found in his work, even as in the great critic's life. Modern instances of literary biography, such as Richard Ellmann's lives of W. B. Yeats, James Joyce, and Oscar Wilde, essentially follow in Boswell's pattern.

That the writer somehow is in the work, we need not doubt, though with William Shakespeare, writer-of-writers, we almost always need to rely upon pure surmise. The exquisite rancidities of the Problem Plays or Dark Comedies seem to express an extraordinary estrangement of Shakespeare from himself. When we read or attend *Troilus and Cressida* and *Measure for Measure*, we may be startled by particular speeches of Ulysses in the first play, or of Vincentio in the second. These speeches, of Ulysses upon hierarchy or upon time, or of Duke Vincentio upon death, are too strong either for their contexts or for the characters of their speakers. The same phenomenon occurs with Parolles, the military impostor of *All's Well That Ends Well*. Utterly disgraced, he nevertheless affirms: "Simply the thing I am/Shall make me live."

In Shakespeare, more even than in his peers, Dante and Cervantes, meaning always starts itself again through excess or overflow. The strongest of Shakespeare's creatures—Falstaff, Hamlet, Iago, Lear, Cleopatra—have an exuberance that is fiercer than their plays can contain. If Ben Jonson was at all correct in his complaint that "Shakespeare wanted art," it could have been only in a sense that he may not have intended. Where do the personalities of Falstaff or Hamlet touch a limit? What was it in Shakespeare that made the two parts of *Henry IV* and *Hamlet* into "plays unlimited"? Neither Falstaff nor Hamlet will be stopped: their wit, their beautiful, laughing speech, their intensity of being—all these are virtually infinite.

In what ways do Falstaff and Hamlet manifest the writer in the work? Evidently, we can never know, or know enough to answer with any authority. But what would happen if we reversed the question, and asked: How did the work form the writer, Shakespeare?

Of Shakespeare's inwardness, his biography tells us nothing. And yet, to an astonishing extent, Shakespeare created our inwardness. At the least, we can speculate that Shakespeare so lived his life as to conceal the depths of his nature, particularly as he rather prematurely aged. We do not have Shakespeare on Shakespeare, as any good reader of the Sonnets comes to realize: they do not constitute a key that unlocks his heart. No sequence of sonnets could be less confessional or more powerfully detached from the poet's self.

The German poet and universal genius, Goethe, affords a superb contrast to Shakespeare. Of Goethe's life, we know more than everything; I wonder sometimes if we know as much about Napoleon or Freud or any other human being who ever has lived, as we know about Goethe. Everywhere, we can find Goethe in his work, so much so that Goethe seems to crowd the writing out, just as Byron and Oscar Wilde seem to usurp their own literary accomplishments. Goethe, cunning beyond measure, nevertheless invested a rival exuberance in his greatest works that could match his personal charisma. The sublime outrageousness of the Second Part of *Faust*, or of the greater lyric and meditative poems, form a Counter-Sublime to Goethe's own daemonic intensity.

Goethe was fascinated by the daemonic in himself; we can doubt that Shakespeare had any such interests. Evidently, Shakespeare abandoned his acting career just before he composed *Measure for Measure* and *Othello*. I surmise that the egregious interventions by Vincentio and Iago displace the actor's energies into a new kind of mischief-making, a fresh opening to a subtler playwriting-within-the-play.

But what had opened Shakespeare to this new awareness? The answer is the work in the writer, *Hamlet* in Shakespeare. One can go further: it was not so much the play, *Hamlet*, as the character Hamlet, who changed Shakespeare's art forever.

Hamlet's personality is so large and varied that it rivals Goethe's own. Ironically Goethe's Faust, his Hamlet, has no personality at all, and is as colorless as Shakespeare himself seems to have chosen to be. Yet nothing could be more colorful than the Second Part of *Faust*, which is peopled by an astonishing array of monsters, grotesque devils, and classical ghosts.

A contrast between Shakespeare and Goethe demonstrates that in each—but in very different ways—we can better find the work in the person, than we can discover that banal entity, the person in the work. Goethe to many of his contemporaries, seemed to be a mortal god. Shakespeare, so far as we know, seemed an affable, rather ordinary fellow, who aged early and became somewhat withdrawn. Yet Faust, though Mephistopheles battles for his soul, is hardly worth the trouble unless you take him as an idea and not as a person. Hamlet is nearly every-idea-in-one, but he is precisely a personality and a person.

Would Hamlet be so astonishingly persuasive if his father's ghost did not haunt him? Falstaff is more alive than Prince Hal, who says that the devil haunts him in the shape of an old fat man. Three years before composing the final *Hamlet*, Shakespeare invented Falstaff, who then never ceased to haunt his creator. Falstaff and Hamlet may be said to best represent the work in the writer, because their influence upon Shakespeare was prodigious. W.H. Auden accurately observed that Falstaff possesses infinite energy: never tired, never bored, and absolutely both witty and happy until Hal's rejection destroys him. Hamlet too has infinite energy, but in him it is more curse than blessing.

Falstaff and Hamlet can be said to occupy the roles in Shakespeare's invented world that Sancho Panza and Don Quixote possess in Cervantes's. Shakespeare's plays from 1610 on (starting with *Twelfth Night*) are thus analogous to the Second Part of Cervantes's epic novel. Sancho and the Don overtly jostle Cervantes for authorship in the Second Part, even as Cervantes battles against the impostor who has pirated a continuation of his work. As a dramatist, Shakespeare manifests the work in the writer more indirectly. Falstaff's prose genius is revived in the scapegoating of Malvolio by Maria and Sir Toby Belch, while Falstaff's darker insights are developed by Feste's melancholic wit. Hamlet's intellectual resourcefulness, already deadly, becomes poisonous in Iago and in Edmund. Yet we have not crossed into the deeper abysses of the work in the writer in later Shakespeare.

No fictive character, before or since, is Falstaff's equal in self-trust. Sir John, whose delight in himself is contagious, has total confidence both in his self-awareness and in the resources of his language. Hamlet, whose self is as strong, and whose language is as copious, nevertheless distrusts both the self and language. Later Shakespeare is, as it were, much under the influence both of Falstaff and of Hamlet, but they tug him in opposite directions. Shakespeare's own copiousness of language is well-nigh incredible: a vocabulary in excess of twenty-one thousand words, almost eighteen hundred of which he coined himself. And of his word-hoard, nearly half are used only once each, as though the perfect setting for each had been found, and need not be repeated. Love for language and faith in language are Falstaffian attributes. Hamlet will darken both that love and that faith in Shakespeare, and perhaps the Sonnets can best be read as Falstaff and Hamlet counterpointing against one another.

Can we surmise how aware Shakespeare was of Falstaff and Hamlet, once they had played themselves into existence? *Henry IV, Part I* appeared in six quarto editions during Shakespeare's lifetime; *Hamlet* possibly had four. Falstaff and Hamlet were played again and again at the Globe, but Shakespeare knew also that they were being read, and he must have had contact with some of those readers. What would it have been like to discuss Falstaff or Hamlet with one of their early readers (presumably also part of their audience at the Globe), if you were the creator of such demiurges? The question would seem nonsensical to most Shakespeare scholars, but then these days they tend to be either ideologues or moldy figs. How can we recover the uncanniness of Falstaff and of Hamlet, when they now have become so familiar?

A writer's influence upon himself is an unexplored problem in criticism, but such an influence is never free from anxieties. The biocritical problem (which this series attempts to explore) can be divided into two areas, difficult to disengage fully. Accomplished works affect the author's life, and also affect her subsequent writings. It is simpler for me to surmise the effect of *Mrs. Dalloway* and *To the Lighthouse* upon Woolf's late *Between the Acts*, than it is to relate Clarissa Dalloway's suicide and Lily Briscoe's capable endurance in art to the tragic death and complex life of Virginia Woolf.

There are writers whose lives were so vivid that they seem sometimes to obscure the literary achievement: Byron, Wilde, Malraux, Hemingway. But most major Western writers do not live that exuberantly, and the greatest of all, Shakespeare, sometimes appears to have adopted the personal mask of colorlessness. And yet there are heroes of literature who struggled titanically with their own eras—Tolstoy, Milton, Victor Hugo—who nevertheless matter more for their works than their lives.

There are great figures—Emily Dickinson, Wallace Stevens, Willa Cather—who seem to have had so little of the full intensity of life when compared to the vitality of their work, that we might almost speak of the work in the work, rather than even of the work in a person. Emily Brontë might well be the extreme instance of such a visionary, surpassing William Blake in that one regard.

I conclude this general introduction to a series of literary bio-critiques by stating a tentative formula or principle for gauging the many ways in which the work influences the person and her subsequent, later work. Our influence upon ourselves is always related to the Shakespearean invention of self-overhearing, which I have written about in several other contexts. Life, as well as poetry and prose, is overheard rather than simply heard. The writer listens to herself as though she were somebody else, and the will to change begins to operate. The forces that live in us include the prior work we have done, and the dreams and waking visions that evade our dismissals.

HAROLD BLOOM

Introduction

There are certain great poets with harsh, recalcitrant personalities: Dante, Milton, Wordsworth. Their antithesis can be found in the geniuses of geniality: Chaucer, Goethe, Heine. Shakespeare, from what we know, was amiable but reserved. A Bio-Critical view of Wordsworth, the greatest of modern poets in English, ought to start with his difficult personal nature.

Wordsworth's mother died when he was eight, his father when he was thirteen. He was "left alone with the visible world," and re-begot himself, seeing himself as nature's child. Beware of nature's children: self-centered, they live for themselves and convert others to living for them. Those who lived for Wordsworth included his sister, Dorothy; his best friend, Samuel Taylor Coleridge; his wife Mary Hutchinson, and sister-in-law Sara Hutchinson (whom Coleridge loved in vain); and to some extent Annette Vallon, his lover in France whom he abandoned, with their daughter Caroline.

Nothing is got from nothing, and after his great poetic decade of 1797–1807, Wordsworth iced over. There are a few exceptions, but fundamentally the Laureate Wordsworth spent the years 1808–1850 writing bad poetry.

Ralph Waldo Emerson, who was not amused, recalled a pilgrimage to Wordsworth during which he was walked back and forth in the garden for some hours, while Wordsworth chanted Wordsworth from memory.

Still, the negativity of Wordsworth's nature, however sublime in its egotism (a complaint of Keats and Shelley) is simply what might be

1

termed the cost of his confirmation. Turn from Wordsworth the man to Wordsworth the poet, and you hear John Milton born again:

> So prayed, more gaining than he asked, the Bard—
> In holiest mood. Urania, I shall need
> Thy guidance, or a greater Muse, if such
> Descend to earth or dwell in highest heaven!
> For I must tread on shadowy ground, must sink
> Deep—and, aloft ascending, breathe in worlds
> To which the heaven of heavens is but a veil.
> All strength—all terror, single or in bands,
> That ever was put forth in personal form—
> Jehovah—with his thunder, and the choir
> Of shouting Angels, and the empyreal thrones—
> I pass them unalarmed. Not Chaos, not
> The darkest pit of lowest Erebus,
> Nor aught of blinder vacancy, scooped out
> By help of dreams—can breed such fear and awe
> As fall upon us often when we look
> Into our Minds, into the Mind of Man—
> My haunt, and the main region of my song.
> —Beauty—a living Presence of the earth,
> Surpassing the most fair ideal Forms
> Which craft of delicate Spirits hath composed
> From earth's materials—waits upon my steps;
> Pitches her tents before me as I move,
> An hourly neighbour. Paradise, and groves
> Elysian, Fortunate Fields—like those of old
> Sought in the Atlantic Main—why should they be
> A history only of departed things,
> Or a mere fiction of what never was?
> For the discerning intellect of Man,
> When wedded to this goodly universe
> In love and holy passion, shall find these
> A simple produce of the common day.

Overtly, these lines offer a greater-than-Milton, who will reject all mythologies in the name of "a simple produce of the common day." Everything before Wordsworth is rejected as a fiction: he comes to offer us the truth of our own nature. His formidable personality will not charm us, but he will make poetry itself new, as though he came alone to cleanse it, and us.

DALE ANDERSON

Biography of William Wordsworth

A MEETING OF MINDS

On June 5, 1797, Samuel Taylor Coleridge took a fateful walk. Coleridge was a struggling young writer full of enthusiasm, passionate about literature and about the people he admired. In 1797, two of his current enthusiasms were walking the English countryside and appreciating the talent of another young poet, William Wordsworth. Coleridge had read some of Wordsworth's poems and already considered him "the best poet of our age." Wordsworth likewise thought highly of Coleridge. "His talent appears to me very great," he had written to a friend. They had met two years before, and since then had traded several letters discussing poetry. Now Coleridge was in western England, near where Wordsworth and his sister Dorothy were renting a country house. He determined to spend some time with his fellow poet so he could get to know him better and talk more deeply about their ideas. Setting out from Bristol, he trudged for several days to reach Wordsworth's home near the town of Crewkerne.

On the afternoon of June 5, Coleridge neared Racedown Lodge, the home where the Wordsworths were living. As he reached the top of a hill, he saw the house. The poet and his sister were working in the garden. Thrilled, Coleridge leaped over the fence that lined the road. Then, as Dorothy later recalled, he "bounded down a pathless field," striding quickly through growing wheat to reach them.

Soon after Coleridge's arrival, Wordsworth read him a new poem he had been working on. Coleridge was impressed to call it "one of the most beautiful poems in the language." After the reading, the three took a break to enjoy afternoon tea. Then it was Coleridge's turn to impress the Wordsworths. He recited two acts of a verse drama he was writing. Wordsworth apparently spoke approvingly of it. Two days later, Coleridge wrote to a publisher friend, "Wordsworth admires my tragedy—which gives me great hopes."

Coleridge stayed the night. The next day, Wordsworth read to his friend from a verse play of his own. Coleridge was thrilled. "His drama is absolutely wonderful," he wrote. "There are in the piece those profound touches of the human heart which I find ... often in Shakespeare." A few weeks later, he wrote glowingly about Wordsworth to another friend: "Wordsworth is a very great man, the only man to whom at all times and in all modes of excellence I feel myself inferior."

Coleridge stayed again that night—and several more. In fact, he lingered at Racedown Lodge for as long as two weeks. He stayed even though he had a wife and baby boy at home. During those days, he and the Wordsworths talked about poetry, politics, and religion. They discussed life, society, and nature. They took walks—for the Wordsworths, like Coleridge, greatly enjoyed a vigorous walk. The days were a delight to the two poets and to Dorothy. She wrote to a friend that Coleridge's "conversation teems with soul, mind, and spirit." Coleridge admired her as well.

The three became fast friends—literary soul-mates. By mid-July, Wordsworth and Dorothy had left Racedown to move to another country house, named Alfoxden. A major appeal of this new home was that it was only three miles from Coleridge and his family. They met daily, with either Coleridge visiting Alfoxden or the Wordsworths visiting him and his family. They took long walks in the countryside, admiring the natural beauty they appreciated. They talked passionately about poetry and traded suggestions on how to improve their two plays. They spoke eagerly of getting those plays produced in London, and made plans to travel together to Germany. In the spring of 1798, they began working together on a new volume of poetry.

Coleridge's June 1797 visit to Racedown Lodge launched a deep and important friendship. That friendship did more than provide the two poets with pleasant company or the exciting exchange of ideas—it profoundly shaped their careers. Coleridge's encouragement and admiration had a tremendous impact on Wordsworth, helping him to confirm his recent decision to pursue a career as a writer. Coleridge's philosophical views shaped Wordsworth's thinking, and his energetic mind helped stimulate Wordsworth to a flurry of creativity. In early 1798, Wordsworth churned out several poems to fill the book of poetry that the two were planning. This work included some experiments with new forms of poetry. It also included "Tintern Abbey," one of his first great poems.

Coleridge's friendship had a more lasting impact on Wordsworth as well. It was this fellow poet who urged Wordsworth to begin a long poem that explored human life, nature, and philosophy. In the end, Wordsworth was unable to complete this massive project. But he finished an important part, the epic-length poem titled *The Prelude, or Growth of a Poet's Mind.* In its thousands of lines, Wordsworth probed the influences and ideas that formed his life in beautiful language that still moves readers today.

In short, Coleridge's 1797 visit helped make Wordsworth one of the most skillful and deeply thoughtful poets of the English language. *Lyrical Ballads*, the book of poems that Coleridge and Wordsworth published in 1798, changed the course of English poetry for decades to come.

WORDSWORTH THE CHILD

William Wordsworth was born on April 7, 1770 in the town of Cockermouth in Cumberland County. Cumberland and two other counties in the northwest of England—Westmoreland and Lancashire—make up a region called the Lake District. The name comes from the fifteen beautiful lakes that dot the area. Among them is Windermere, England's largest lake.

The Cumbrian mountains also rise in this region, boldly pushing to the sky. While not as lofty as Europe's Alps or America's Rockies, these mountains maintain an imposing presence. In the late 1700s, when Wordsworth was born, much of England had been settled for hundreds of years. The land had been turned into farms or grazing areas or taken by growing cities. The Lake District stood out as one of the country's remaining wild places. Here a person could hike up mountains or around lakes and feel in touch with nature.

Wordsworth was a lover of natural beauty and the Lake District provided a perfect home for his soul—and a spur to his art. Wordsworth visited many parts of Great Britain and the European continent during his life yet he felt most at home in the Lake District. In one of his earliest poems, "An Evening Walk," he describes the area as having "the sweep of endless woods, / Blue pomp of lakes, high cliffs and falling floods." At night, he says, the lakes shine like a "burnished mirror" to reflect the stars, a "thousand thousand twinkling points of light." Not surprisingly, he spent almost his entire life in this region. He lived there from birth to age 17 and from age 29 until he died.

Wordsworth's parents were John Wordsworth and Ann Cookson Wordsworth. His father—29-years-old when William was born—worked as the local agent and personal lawyer of Sir James Lowther, Earl of Lonsdale. At this point in British history, Parliament seats were decided by election, and nobles like Lowther used agents to manipulate voters to support the candidate of their choosing. The candidate in turn reinforced the power of the lord.

Sir James Lowther's use of this practice had earned him a particularly poor reputation. In the words of one observer, he was "more detested than any man alive." Unfortunately for the Wordsworth family, popular feeling against the lord was also directed at his agent, John Wordsworth. In her teens, Dorothy Wordsworth noted that "amongst all those who visited at my father's house he had not one real friend."

Some of that ill feeling derived from Wordsworth's mother's family as well. Her father—the poet's maternal grandfather—ran a business that sold cloth while her mother was from the noble Crackanthorpe family. The Crackanthorpes looked down on John Wordsworth. Similarly, the Cooksons did not approve of him, and both families opposed Sir James Lowther. As a result, relations between the families of the poet's mother and father were not good.

William was the second of five children. Brother Richard, who later became a lawyer, was two years older. Sister Dorothy, with whom William was extremely close, was born in 1771 followed by the birth of Brother John in 1772 and brother Christopher in 1774. John later became a sailor and Christopher a scholar.

The Wordsworths lived in the most impressive house in Cockermouth. The two-story building stood behind a stone wall with a commanding gate. Behind the house, a garden stretched down to the River Derwent. The house came with John Wordsworth's job, but the Wordsworth children did not enjoy it. It was less a home than a place of business and politics for their father. People came and went frequently, disrupting whatever routine Ann Wordsworth tried to arrange for her children. In addition, their father often had to be away from home on Lord Lowther's business.

For these reasons, Ann Wordsworth and her children spent a great deal of time at her parents' home in Penrith. The mother no doubt enjoyed receiving some help in raising five young children. But the children strongly felt that their grandparents did not love them because of their father.

Young William, whose passion was to wander outside, did not wish to stay long in either house. In his autobiographical poem *The Prelude*, Wordsworth happily remembers swimming in the nearby water, lazing about in the sun, roaming over fields, or scampering up rocks. His early schooling was haphazard—as living in more than one home made it difficult to have a well-organized education. Among his early schooling, he attended classes at Ann Birkett's school in Penrith, where his future wife, Mary Hutchinson, was also a pupil, but his education was not well-rounded. Later in life, he did credit one of these early schools for helping to train his powerful memory. In academics, however, the instruction was light. At age nine, he was sent to a well-known school in the town of Hawkshead. There, he later recalled, he learned more Latin in two weeks than he had in the previous two years.

One thing he did learn at home was to appreciate poetry. His father, early on, required him to memorize poems or parts of poems. William dutifully committed to memory poems by William Shakespeare and John Milton—even though their language and ideas were quite complex for a child. The exercise paid off in many ways. First, it helped him develop a powerful memory. Throughout his life, he could remember lines of poetry that he had read or heard just once decades before. Also, relying on that powerful memory became the very basis of his art. Many of Wordsworth's greatest poems are built on his ability to describe the emotions he remembers at specific times in his past. Finally, Wordsworth's early exposure to great poetry most likely shaped his decision to become a poet and influenced his skill as a writer. Many of his most skillful poems are written in the blank verse—poetry that does not rhyme—like much of Shakespeare and Milton. And his best poems reflect the power and imagination of those great writers.

Though Wordsworth's memory was powerful, he had few recollections of his mother, who died in 1778 of pneumonia when he was only eight. At least, he had few that he admitted to. He speaks of her warmly as "the heart / And hinge of all our leaving and our loves."

Ann Wordsworth's death disrupted the family in many ways. John Wordsworth found it difficult to care for five children ranging from ages four to ten—especially when he was away from home so often. As a result, Wordsworth's beloved sister Dorothy was sent to live with one set of relations in central England; they would not see each other for eight years. William and his elder brother Richard were sent to the grammar school at Hawkshead, in the southern part of the Lake District. When they were old enough, brothers John and Christopher joined them there.

The Hawkshead School had been in existence for nearly 200 years when William and Richard Wordsworth enrolled. The school had an excellent reputation for preparing students for university, and at the time of their admittance, about a hundred students attended. The setting was not in the most scenic area of the Lake District, but one of the lakes was close by, and two more—including Windermere—were not far away.

Wordsworth loved the area. During the eight years he spent at the school, he enjoyed roaming over the hills, rocks, and lakes around Hawkshead. He and the other boys swam or boated in the lake, climbed, and collected nuts in the woods. They fished and caught woodcocks—game birds they could sell at the market. They sometimes clambered high over the rocks to find the nests of ravens. Then they destroyed the eggs—people hated the ravens for attacking their animals. They skated in the winter. This was a pastime Wordsworth enjoyed even when he was 60.

Often Wordsworth enjoyed these activities with other students. One of his delights was to walk the five-mile route around Esthwaite Water, the nearby lake, early in the morning. He often did this with his closest friend, John Fleming. They recited nature poems as they walked. Sometimes they composed new verses of their own, making up poems as they trudged along. But Wordsworth also enjoyed setting out alone. Sometimes he sat upon a rock above the lake simply to enjoy the stillness. He later described in *The Prelude* how he loved being at the lake "at the first hour of morning, when the vale / Lay quiet in an utter solitude."

As he matured, Wordsworth showed great curiosity. One older schoolmate remembered him as "always asking him questions about one thing or another." But his questions were not only aimed at school subjects. He enjoyed talking to the workers in the area. The region had coal mines and slate quarries, and an iron foundry nearby. There was lumbering to provide wood for charcoal to fuel the foundry. Workers carted goods into and out of the valley every week. It was a busy place, and Wordsworth was interested in the people and their stories, many of which found their way into his poetry.

The two Hawkshead people that Wordsworth was closest to were probably Ann and Hugh Tyson. The Wordsworth boys did not live in the school but in the cottage of this couple, who were in their mid-sixties when William and Richard first arrived in 1779. They had no children of their own but were kind-hearted and generous to the brothers. Wordsworth loved Ann Tyson as the kindly grandmother he had never had. He declared that love in *The Prelude:*

> The thoughts of gratitude shall fall like dew
> Upon thy grave, good creature: while my heart
> Can beat I never will forget thy name.
> Heaven's blessing be upon thee.

The Wordsworth boys stayed with the Tysons most of the year. They had a two-week holiday at Christmas, when they went home to their father at Cockermouth. During the six- to eight-week summer vacation, they alternated between their father and their mother's family at Penrith.

Most of the year, of course, was taken up by studies. Students at Hawkshead learned the Classical languages, and Wordsworth's love for Latin continued into adulthood. They studied science and mathematics, and learned English grammar and composition—the craft of writing. Wordsworth took supplementary classes outside school to learn French and dancing.

Two of his teachers were particularly interested in poetry, and taught more than the established poets Shakespeare and Milton. They made sure that their students read widely in the newer poets whose work reflected an interest in nature, including John Dyer, James Thompson, and Thomas Gray. Though their neoclassical style was far different from the moving lyrical voice of Wordsworth's later poetry, these were the poets whose work influenced Wordsworth and his friend John Fleming so greatly as they rambled in the English countryside.

The schoolmaster, William Taylor, also challenged his students to write their own poetry. Wordsworth was eager to take on the challenge. He had, in fact, begun composing poems on his own. Later in life, Wordsworth pointed to his years at Hawkshead as the time when he decided to dedicate himself to poetry. He dated the decision to 1783 or 1784, when he was 14. Three years later, he had a poem published in *European Magazine*.

The winter of 1783–1784 brought Wordsworth two powerful occurrences. The first came late in 1783. He and brothers Richard and Christopher returned home for Christmas. They discovered their father seriously ill and fading fast. By December 30, he was dead. The five Wordsworth children were now orphans. They were also without a home, which all the Wordsworth children felt acutely. Wordsworth later recalled the painful feeling: "homeless near a thousand homes I stood."

Uncles Richard Wordsworth and Christopher Crackanthorpe became their guardians. They quickly sold the family's possessions and all the land that John Wordsworth had owned, which produced about £10,000. The sum could support the children for some time, but it was not enough to pay for college for the boys. (In this period, there was no chance for Dorothy to attend college.) The eldest, Richard, was studying law with his uncle, a barrister.

There might have been more money, but a review of accounts revealed that John Wordsworth had spent nearly £4,500 of his own money on behalf of Lord Lowther. For two years, the guardian uncles gathered evidence of these expenses. When they presented it to Lowther, his lordship simply refused to repay the money. The Wordsworths were forced to bring a lawsuit to collect the funds. Since Lowther had political power, they were not at all certain to win the suit. In the meantime, the two uncles generously agreed to pay for the cost of college for William and Christopher, the best students out of the four boys. The uncles hoped that when the suit was finally settled, the college costs would be repaid.

The second incident in the winter of 1783–1784 was another death. On the last day of February, 1784, Hugh Tyson died. In two short months, the Wordsworth boys had lost their father and the man who had been like a grandfather to them.

Still, William survived these cruel blows and continued studying at Hawkshead for three more years. In 1787, he graduated. When the school year ended, he and his brothers prepared to return to Penrith for the summer. But uncle Christopher Crackanthorpe rudely sent no horse or carriage to carry his nephews home. William had to hire a horse at his own expense. It was not a promising beginning to the summer.

There was good news when they arrived, though. His sister Dorothy was to spend the summer at Penrith also. It was the Wordsworth children's first time together after eight years, and William and Dorothy were thrilled to see each other. The two had been very close—and would remain so for the rest of their lives. In this summer, they talked deeply about their difficult circumstances, and shared news of their experiences and reading. And, of course, they enjoyed many fine walks in the country. On some of these walks, they were joined by their friend Mary Hutchinson, whom they had known for many years.

On the whole, though, the summer was unpleasant. Relations between the Wordsworth children and their extended family were cool. In a letter to a friend, Dorothy complained that their grandparents constantly scolded them. Even the servants made their lives difficult. Uncle Christopher, she added, "[had] taken a dislike" to William. The situation grew so difficult that William left before the college year began. He traveled to Hawkshead, where he spent several weeks at Ann Tyson's home. Her loving care no doubt soothed his ruffled feelings.

STUDENT AND REPUBLICAN

In the fall of 1787, Wordsworth reached Cambridge, where he would begin college. The school was not yet a university, but a collection of sixteen colleges. Among them were Trinity College, once home to the scientist Isaac Newton; Christ's, where poet John Milton had studied; and Jesus, which Coleridge would enter in 1791. Wordsworth joined St. John's College. His entrance there was secured by William Cookson, his mother's brother. Cookson had attended St. John's and in the 1780s served as one of the more than fifty fellows who ran it.

Cookson expected that Wordsworth—an excellent student—would follow the path he himself had taken. He would earn his bachelor's degree with honors and then win one of the fellowships set aside for students from Cumberland. While a fellow, he would study for his master's degree and wait for a position in the clergy to open. When it did, he would take the post, marry, and settle down to a respectable, conservative life as a clergyman.

Cookson was in a position to make this happen for his nephew. He was currently one of the college's fellows and expected to receive a clergy position soon, and could use his influence to keep the fellowship open until Wordsworth graduated. He was a friend to William Wilberforce, a politician who was close to William Pitt, England's prime minister. And Cookson knew King George III because he had helped teach the King's sons. Cookson could almost guarantee this path to a career for Wordsworth. But Wordsworth was not convinced he wanted that life.

Wordsworth had another relation with ideas for his future. John Robinson, a cousin of his father, was also a well-connected politician. He, too, knew the King and Pitt. With his friends, he could also help Wordsworth launch a safe and successful career after graduation. He advised Wordsworth to make the most of his college years. "Establish a reputation at College which will go with you, and serve you [throughout] life," he wrote in a letter. He urged Wordsworth to become a "wrangler," or one of the students with top honors. (The name came from the top students' skill at debating, or wrangling.) At first, this idea seemed to appeal to Wordsworth. On his way to Cambridge, he stopped one night at the house of Robinson's brother. "I shall either be senior wrangler," Wordsworth promised Robinson's brother, "or nothing!"

He had the background and the ability to do it. His solid education at Hawkshead had prepared him well. When he arrived at college, he found himself fully a year ahead of many fellow students in mathematics. Two months after arriving at Cambridge, he had his first exams. He passed them easily, placing in the top group of honors students.

Wordsworth quickly lost interest in academic distinctions, however. The one-year head-start he enjoyed in mathematics when he arrived apparently evaporated. In a letter to a friend, Dorothy suggested the reason. Her brother "never opens a mathematical book," she wrote. He attended classes, but he did not push himself. By the exams of June 1788, he had slipped to second-level honors.

He did plenty of reading, though. He continued studying the Classical authors that he loved. He took up Italian and read important Italian authors in the original language. And he enjoyed what he called "lazy reading"—books he read for pleasure, not because they were required for courses. Some of these authors were newer poets and novelists who were not taught at the college. But he also spent time with such major writers in the English canon as Geoffrey Chaucer.

In his second year at Cambridge, Wordsworth began working on a poem, which he finished the following year. "An Evening Walk" is one of his first extensive writings—the poem reaches nearly 400 lines. It is a type of poem common in the late eighteenth-century in which a poet describes the geography of a place. In this case, the place is the Lake District. He wrote the poem in couplets—pairs of lines that rhyme with each other—rather than the unrhymed blank verse that he used for many of his greatest poems. The poem reveals that in his Cambridge years, Wordsworth missed two things dearly: his beloved Lake District, where he felt most at home, and his sister Dorothy, to whom the poem is addressed.

Distance from the lakes and from Dorothy did not prevent him from having fun at college, though. Reflecting back on this time in *The Prelude*, he admitted that he was always ready to enjoy himself—"my heart / Was social and loved idleness and joy." As an older adult, Wordsworth seemed a bit stuffy and overly serious. As a college man, though, he was far more relaxed and gregarious.

Wordsworth took part in many distractions standard for college students of the period. He boated on the Cam River, read newspapers in coffee houses, and argued endlessly with fellow students. He managed to avoid the fights that often broke out between the college students and the young men of the town of Cambridge, but he was a willing participant in student parties. Many of these parties included drinking contests. At one, Wordsworth drank a few too many toasts to poet John Milton, and ended up extremely drunk. When the bells sounded calling the students to chapel, he had to race to the church, comically pulling his student gown over his head as he ran.

During summer vacations, Wordsworth avoided his mother's family. Rather than traveling to Penrith, he spent the summers of 1788 and 1789 at Ann Tyson's home near Hawkshead. He did visit his uncle Crackanthorpe, but his stays were brief. The following summer, he and fellow student Robert Jones embarked on a journey that would prove a major influence in his poetry and, in particular, his philosophy of poetry. Between June and September, he and Jones traveled to the European continent, where they walked nearly 3,000 miles through France,

Switzerland, and northern Italy. They covered 20 to 30 miles a day, even though much of the journey was over mountainous terrain. They kept constantly on the move, rarely spending more than one night at a stopping place. The two travelers wrapped their few possessions in a cloth, which they put on top of their heads. The sight, Wordsworth admitted, "contributes not a little to that general curiosity which we seem to excite."

Their chief goal of this trip was to take in the beautiful scenery of Switzerland's mountains, the Alps. Hiking through the mountains moved Wordsworth deeply. In a letter to Dorothy, he described the "terrible majesty" of the mountains. "I had not a thought of man," he wrote, "or a single created being." Instead, he thought of the power of God. These treks through the high mountain passes in one of the largest mountain ranges on earth were the birth place of Wordsworth's aesthetic view of poetry, in particular "the sublime." He recounts their journey over the Simplon pass in the *Prelude* VII.

This trek through Europe required good planning and an impressive amount of energy. It was remarkable for another reason, though. Wordsworth and Jones made the trip in the midst of great turmoil in France, where the Revolution had begun a year earlier. Though the French Revolution had not yet entered its bloodiest stage, the situation was unstable. Louis XVI still ruled in name, but it was the National Assembly who wielded the real power in government. Fortunately for the two Englishmen, they were heartily cheered everywhere in France. Many French admired how the English had managed in the 1600s to limit the power of their king.

In truth, the two travelers took little notice of events in France. Their brisk pace carried them through France very quickly, and they marched on a straight route from Calais, where they landed, to southern France. This route kept them away from Paris, where much of the revolutionary action was. Besides this, Wordsworth was far more interested in Swiss politics than French—Switzerland had been a republic for many decades. This reason, as much as the desire to see the Alps, made Switzerland his chief destination.

The trip to Europe revealed that Wordsworth had abandoned uncle Cookson's plans for him. To get the fellowship he was supposed to earn, he should have spent the summer in Cambridge in a study group. Instead, he chose the walking tour.

In the fall of 1790, the travelers returned to England. Wordsworth went briefly to Cambridge but only to meet the college's residence requirement that allowed him to take final exams—no classes were required of fourth-year students. To underscore his lack of interest in the upcoming exams, he did no studying for them. Instead, he read novels. At the Christmas holiday, he travelled to his uncle Cookson's, though he had no desire to see him. His uncle, unhappy with his conduct, likewise had little desire to see him. But his desire to see Dorothy, now residing there, persuaded him. The brother and sister spent hours every day walking and talking, as he excitedly related what he had done and seen in Europe. Back at school after the holidays ended, Wordsworth took his exams. He passed and graduated in January 1791—but not with honors, as had been hoped just a few years before. Within days, he left Cambridge for London.

Wordsworth spent four months in England's capital. He had no plan for his life as yet. He spent a great deal of time walking about the city, taking in the sights and meeting people of different trades. He visited booksellers and printers. He attended some of the debates in Parliament, which became heated as the House of Lords began to worry about the course of the Revolution in France. He heard the impassioned speeches of Edmund Burke, Charles James Fox, and Prime Minister William Pitt; Wordsworth admired both the conservative Burke and the more liberal Fox. He recognized the skill of all three politicians, but he also saw differences in how they gained influence. After hearing their speeches, he wrote, a person "always went from Burke with your mind filled; from Fox with your feelings excited; and from Pitt with wonder at his having the power to make the worse [reason] appear the better reason."

By May, Wordsworth was ready to move elsewhere. Robert Jones had invited him to visit Wales. Short of money—and with Parliament shutting down for the summer—Wordsworth decided to go. He stayed for several months, and the two carried out another walking tour, this time of Jones's homeland. A highlight of this trip was the walk up Mount Snowdon, in northwest Wales. While not as high as the mountains of the Alps, Snowdon is an impressive peak. The two friends hoped to reach the summit just as dawn broke. By taking the path they chose, they would be facing in the right direction to see the sunrise. They set out around midnight and climbed for several hours, guided by a local shepherd. But they reached the top too quickly. Emerging from the mist surrounding the mountain, they found not the warm light of the rising sun but the cold moon. Wordsworth later used the experience in *The Prelude.* In it, he compared the power of the imagination to the light of the moon breaking above the mist.

Wordsworth left Wales in the fall and spent the rest of the year traveling between Cambridge, London, and Bristol. He was in a difficult position, with little money and no sure future. His status was even worse when compared to that of his brothers. Richard was rising in the law, and John, working for the East India Company, was building a successful career at sea. Christopher, still at Cambridge, was applying himself to his studies as William never had. William, on the other hand, was still a drain on the family's finances. The family's suit against Lord Lowther had made some progress. In 1791, the courts had turned down the noble's last attempt to avoid paying the bills owed John Wordsworth. But the court delayed final decision on how much he had to pay. Wordsworth knew he would receive some money, but had no idea how much. In the meantime, his uncles continued to press him to become a clergyman.

Though he had no clear idea of what he wanted to do, Wordsworth resisted this plan, and instead devised a scheme to leave England for a few months. He told his family he would return to Cambridge and undertake more studies and prepare for the clergy. Instead, he set off for France. Wordsworth later said that he simply wanted to learn French more thoroughly. This seems an unconvincing reason. He might have been led there simply to get away from the pressure from his uncles.

Wordsworth was also motivated by a growing interest in the conflict in France. Listening to the debates in Parliament had stimulated his interest in politics, and the Revolution was taking intriguing new turns. By going to France, he could see first-hand the changes taking place. Louis XVI had recently tried to escape from Paris, apparently ready to join the armies of other countries assembled by other rulers in Europe who were interested in protecting the monarchy. These rulers threatened to attack France and restore King Louis to the throne, but he was captured and brought back to Paris. The Revolution's claims to be fighting for the "rights of man" were appealing to an idealistic young man.

Beyond that, the situation in France was somewhat similar to his own. The revolutionaries were trying to tear down an old system in which nobles and church officials had all the power and wealth, forcing others to conform to their will. Wordsworth might have seen parallels in his own life. After all, Lord Lowther had abused his family and was still withholding the money he owed. And his uncles were trying to force him into a career in which he had no interest.

Whatever the causes, Wordsworth set off for France in November 1792. He spent some time in Paris and then moved to Orléans. There, he met Annette Vallon, the twenty-five-year-old daughter of a surgeon. From outward respects, she seemed his opposite. Vallon was full of energy and passion—against the Revolution. She and her family were committed supporters of the king, and two of her cousins belonged to the Catholic clergy. Wordsworth was Protestant. Despite these differences, Wordsworth and Vallon began a close relationship. Wordsworth eventually dropped any pretence that he was in France to learn the language, and simply focused on his time with Annette. Sometime early in 1793, she left Orléans for the family home at Blois. Wordsworth followed her there.

While courting Annette, Wordsworth also spent time with two French republicans, Michel Beaupuy, and army officer, and Henri Grégorie, a Catholic clergymen, both commited to the Revolution. It was Beaupuy, Wordsworth later wrote, who convinced him that the Revolution was desirable because it could end the suffering that the old regime caused for the poor. The cultured and eloquent Grégorie helped persuade Wordsworth that the old regime in France was indeed evil.

Wordsworth also found time in this period to work on another poem, "Descriptive Sketches." This lengthy piece describes what he had seen in his 1790 walk through Europe with Robert Jones. Like "An Evening Walk," it was written in rhyming couplets, and it also followed some of the conventions of eighteenth-century landscape poetry. The poem ends with something that reflects Wordsworth's thinking at the time: he closes by begging God to let "Freedom's waves" ride over all the evils of the old monarchical system. Those evils include conquest, greed, pride, famine, oppression, persecution, and ambition.

As the months passed, problems arose. One was personal—Annette became pregnant. Another was financial—Wordsworth was running out of money. A third was political—the Revolution began to take a darker turn. A Parisian mob attacked and massacred some of the king's guards, and soon after, the National Assembly ordered the king arrested and abolished the monarchy. New laws made life dangerous for members of the clergy—including Annette's cousins—and for foreigners. Another mob broke into the prisons of Paris and killed hundreds of people, some who opposed the Revolution and some who were simply innocent victims.

Annette's family worried about her condition and the growing unrest. They might have been upset about their daughter's affair with a Protestant republican, as well. Without telling Wordsworth, they took her from Blois back to Orléans. This city was staunchly royalist, making it safer for the family.

Strapped for support, Wordsworth was forced to write to his brother Richard. After receiving funds, he returned to Paris, though his purpose was not clear. A few weeks later, he asked for money again. This time, though, his uncles blocked any further aid. By the end of the year, Wordsworth was forced to return to England because he lacked the funds to stay in France. About the same time, on December 15, Anne-Caroline Wordsworth, was born. In the document recording her baptism, her father's last name—an English name strange to French ears—was misspelled three times.

What, exactly, Wordsworth's intentions were for Annette Vallon is not clear. It is clear, however, that Vallon hoped to marry him, as she states in a letter of early 1793. No return letters have survived, however. Whatever Wordsworth said to her is unknown. His autobiographical poem *The Prelude* does nothing to reveal his feelings, either. The poem discusses his visit to France and the turmoil of the Revolution. But it makes no mention of Wordsworth's affair with Annette. Instead, it includes a fictional story of a French man, Vaudracour, and a woman, Julia, who love each other passionately. They, too, have a child and suffer the pressures of family opposition. In the poem, their story ends tragically. Julia and the child die, and Vaudracour goes insane. Fortunately for Wordsworth and Annette Vallon, truth was less disastrous than fiction.

Aimless Years

Back in England, Wordsworth had to decide what to do. He needed money—he was, after all, a father now. During his stay in France, he had finally given in and asked his Uncle, William Cookson, to help him secure a position as a clergyman. He did so reluctantly, as he told a friend in a letter: "Had it been in my power I certainly should have wished to defer the moment."

Within a few months time, though, that opportunity was gone because Cookson determined he would not help Wordsworth. The reason is not exactly known, but there were plenty of things he could have objected to in his nephew's actions: his refusal to push himself to excel at his studies, his decision to travel to France instead of furthering his career, his relationship with Annette Vallon. The crux of these was, of course, the issue of his illegitimate daughter. Men intended for the clergy were supposed to avoid sexual relations until they were married. Whatever his uncle's reasoning, Wordsworth could no longer expect help there.

He tried turning to literature. During 1792, he had written a college friend that "the field of Letters is very extensive." He optimistically said that writing could generate enough money "for the necessaries, nay even the comforts of life." To that end, he convinced a London publisher to bring out two of his poems. In 1793, both *An Evening Walk* and *Descriptive Sketches* were published. Sales were poor, and the books did nothing to ease his financial situation. Unknown to Wordsworth, the poems did catch the attention of some other writers, including the young Samuel Taylor Coleridge. For now, though, Wordsworth seemed to be stuck in the same predicament he was in when he returned from France. He was moody and depressed; friends made sure to play cards with him every night in an effort to cheer him up.

Adding to his worries were new political developments in England and France. The Revolution in France had added to the strength of the call for political reform in England. Reformers wanted to give more people the right to vote, and guarantee that Parliament would sit each year. This movement alarmed King George III, who declared it illegal to publish writings that could be labeled seditious. Reformers were closely watched, and one of them—the fiery Thomas Paine—was convicted for his writings in support of the French Revolution. (Paine was convicted *in absentia*; he was in France at the time. He never returned to England.)

Meanwhile, the French Revolution had taken a bloody turn. About the time Wordsworth had left France, King Louis XVI had been tried by a revolutionary court and found guilty of treason. In January 1793, he was executed. The king's execution raised fears in England and elsewhere that France's revolutionary fervor would spread. On February 1, 1793, England declared war on France. War made it even more unlikely that Wordsworth could marry Annette Vallon, even if he wanted to.

The war embittered Wordsworth against his own country. In a passage of *The Prelude*, he describes this alienation; the speaker of the poem sits in a country church feeling alone and angry while the minister and the congregation praise English victories or mourn English losses. Wordsworth, on the other hand, was quite happy when the French armies defeated English troops.

Louix XVI's execution shocked even some in England who had earlier supported the Revolution. One of these early supporters was bishop Richard Watson, who published an angry tract that criticized what was happening in France as "a humiliating picture of human nature." He lauded England as the home of liberty and equality, and said that the English political system was the best that could be found in the world.

The bishop's piece appalled Wordsworth, who wrote a blistering attack. In his response to the bishop, Wordsworth proclaimed that the French had every right to execute the king, and pointed to problems in English government, where elections were far from fair, and the king and the nobles used the law to their own advantage. He argued that English society needed to depose the aristocracy, though he did not urge their execution. He blasted the bishop for unfeeling remarks about the sufferings of England's poor. The tract was a powerful piece of writing. If it saw the light of day, it would probably have been seen as treason. But it was never published, for reasons that remain unclear today. Scholars speculate his publisher might have refused to print it. Or perhaps Wordsworth thought better of putting his name on such an inflammatory document. Either way, the essay was packed away and remained unknown until after Wordsworth's death.

Troubled, Wordsworth decided to leave London to take a tour of western England with a friend. When the carriage they were riding in was destroyed in an accident, the friend abandoned the tour. Wordsworth decided to walk to Robert Jones's home in Wales. To do so, he had to cross Salisbury Plain in southwestern England. It is here that Stonehenge and other ancient stone monuments rise above the flat, treeless land. Wordsworth's walk across the plain was not the pleasant jaunt he enjoyed in the lakes of home or the mountains of Europe, but rather left him unsettled. The weather added to his misery—a hailstorm lashed at him. He stopped to rest one night at Stonehenge. There, according to *The Prelude*, he had a ghastly vision of human sacrifices taking place on the stones. (The belief that Stonehenge had been used for human sacrifice was common at the time.)

Wordsworth also used the walk in another poem, "Salisbury Plain." This poem had nothing in common with his earlier descriptive writings, but tells the story of a man and a woman who both wander the bleak plain looking for shelter in a storm. In this story, Wordsworth expresses some of his anger at the political situation in England. The woman has suffered greatly, her father having been ousted from his home by a more powerful neighbor; her husband, a soldier, was killed in the American Revolution; her children are dead. Despite the bleak circumstances, Wordsworth ends the poem happily, with the two reaching a pleasant valley in a bright morning. He ends with an address to the reader which calls for the victory of freedom over oppression and, as with his response to the bishop, the poem is not published.

Wordsworth did reach Wales and join his friend Jones, but what he did next, in the fall of 1793, is not clear. Some accounts say he remained in England. Others say he took a short, secret trip to France. There he had a brief reunion with Annette Vallon and met his daughter for the first time. Others say that he remained in England. While his whereabouts in late 1793 are unknown, it is clear that by February 1794, he was in Halifax, England, where Dorothy was living. After more than a year of wandering, he needed her comfort and support.

It was at this point that the tide started to turn for Wordsworth. A friend, William Calvert, offered them the use of a farmhouse called Windy Brow, located in the Lake district, and they grabbed at the chance. Dorothy rejoiced in the freedom of living away from relatives and the pleasure of being reunited with her brother. Wordsworth began to calm down and started reworking some of his early poems. He also taught Dorothy Italian and helped her improve her French.

Good fortune came into their lives again. Calvert's younger brother Raisley, living on comfortable allowance, apparently took a liking to Wordsworth's poetry, offering to aid him with financial support. And then he went even further, willing the poet £900. This was more than an empty gesture, because Calvert knew he was dying. Wordsworth spent the fall and early winter caring for his friend, and in January 1795, Calvert died. With his inheritance, Wordsworth had as much as £100 a year available for nine years. Later, he paid tribute to Calvert as one of the three people—Dorothy and Coleridge were the others—who helped make him a poet.

While he was caring for Calvert, Wordsworth carried on a correspondence with his friend William Matthews. They talked about creating a new magazine, titled by Wordsworth *The Philanthropist*. They hoped it would include good literature as well as pieces on politics, philosophy, and other topics. They planned a magazine of "free enquiry"—one in which no subject would be closed out. People were walking "in darkness," Wordsworth told Mathews in one letter, and he vowed to "put into each man's hand a lantern to guide him." In the end, the journal was never published. Wordsworth was derailed by the time spent caring for Raisley Calvert, and Matthews had to take a job to support himself.

It was probably just as well that they dropped the magazine. Many of the ideas they supported were getting heightened attention from the government. New harsh laws were passed, and they could be used punish criticism of the government or calls for reform. Though these views were dangerous, Wordsworth continued to voice them—though not in print. Soon after Calvert died, he returned to London. There he associated with a number of political radicals. Among them was William Godwin, a political thinker who supported many reform causes.

Through these people, Wordsworth made many new acquaintances who would help him in years to come. Godwin introduced him to Basil Montagu, who became a lifelong friend, and Montagu introduced him to Francis Wrangham, who also became a friend for life. Through them both, he met the brothers John and Azariah Pinney. These new friends came to his immediate aid. As Calvert had the year before, they helped the unsettled Wordsworth by offering him a country home they owned, Racedown Lodge, free of rent. It was further arranged that Montagu—whose wife had died—would send his son, Basil, Jr., to the home as well. Wordsworth's sister Dorothy would help with the boy's care and education.

Wordsworth went west to Racedown Lodge, stopping first in Bristol where he met the bookseller John Cottle. He also met two young poets and reformers, Samuel Taylor Coleridge and Robert Southey who were in the midst of planning to form an ideal society named "Pantisocracy." (The name, based on Greek words, meant "a society governed by all the people.") They hoped to plant a new community, perhaps in North America. There, the men and women in the group would live and work together, and there would be no private property and no riches. It is not known whether the two discussed this plan with Wordsworth, but he was impressed with them both. He wrote to William Mathews: "[Coleridge's] talent appears to me very great. I met with Southey also ... and I have every reason to think very highly of his powers of mind."

In September 1795, William and Dorothy Wordsworth moved into Racedown Lodge with young Basil Montagu. The brother and sister were delighted to be together again. In fact, from this time almost until Wordsworth's death, they lived together. This home was a pleasant one, a mansion that had been renovated by the Pinney brothers' wealthy father. It had a huge parlor that stretched from the front of the house to the back. Tucked amid rolling land, it had lovely walks. From the tops of nearby hills, they could see the English Channel.

The brother and sister struggled to get by. Promised payments from Montagu for his son did not always arrive, and prices for food and coal were rising sharply because of the war. They had to resort to gardening to have enough food to eat. Even that was not always successful. Wordsworth wrote a friend jokingly that they were living on "air and the essence of carrots cabbages [and] turnips." Economic troubles and high prices brought suffering to many people in western England. William wrote his friend Mathews that "The country people here are wretchedly poor." From this experience, Wordsworth gained sympathy for the country poor which influenced the poetry that he wrote at Racedown Lodge.

One of his first tasks was to revise the poem about Salisbury Plain. The changes were substantial, making it, as he wrote Wrangham, a completely new poem. In fact, he gave it a new title: "Adventures on Salisbury Plain." He added more characters, each of whom tells a story that explains his or her current miserable condition: a soldier struggling to reach his impoverished daughter; a sailor, forced to a life of crime by a neglectful government; a war widow, bereft of children and home. In the end the sailor turns himself over to authorities and is hanged for his crimes. This bleak and depressing poem reflects Wordsworth's (and his friend Godwin's) growing anger at the injustices they saw in England.

Early in 1796, Wordsworth tried to have the poem published. Coleridge read it and promised it would see print, but neither he nor Joseph Cottle had the money to fund publication. Wordsworth appears not to have minded—he was on to other projects. But Coleridge's praise for the poem was deeply satisfying. It was the first time that he heard a poet he respected judge one of his works so highly.

In the fall, Wordsworth began working on a verse drama called *The Borderers*. It was this play that he read to Coleridge that fateful day two years later. Set in the Middle Ages, it deals with border fighting between England and Scotland. In the play, Wordsworth explores the central question of the French Revolution: is violence in the name of justice justified? Wordsworth shapes the play to make the answer negative. In this, he seems to be rejecting the thinking of Godwin, who had argued that a person should stand up for what he or she believes is right, regardless of society. The play's villain has warped this idea into a justification to base all one's actions on naked self-interest. By linking Godwin's ideas to a completely evil character, Wordsworth discredits the ideas.

Why the change from the attitude of "Adventures on Salisbury Plain"? Wordsworth was still young, only in his early twenties. His philosophy was still forming. He still resented the English government's harsh treatment of dissent and sympathized with the suffering brought on the poor by the war with France. But he also had seen the French Revolution turn from a celebration of liberty and equality to a Reign of Terror. Starting in 1793, Robespierre had taken control of the Revolution, ordering the execution of thousands, including prominent leaders of the earlier stages of the Revolution who had gained Wordsworth's respect.

Later, Wordsworth had another reason for turning against the Revolution. By the late 1790s, France was no longer threatened by invading armies sent by conservative kings who hoped to restore the monarchy. French armies had successfully defended the republic. Then they took the war outside France. French armies became invaders, and in 1798 they invaded Switzerland, the republic that Wordsworth had admired. That France had now become Switzerland's conqueror appalled Wordsworth. It seemed a complete reversal of the ideals that the Revolution had first proclaimed.

Though disillusioned by the Terror, Wordsworth was no happier with England's role in the war. His anger at the war informed his next project as well, the long poem called "The Ruined Cottage." It tells the story of a young couple struggling in the depressed economy of the 1790s. The husband has no choice but to enlist in the army, leaving behind the small sum of money he received as a bonus for joining up. He never returns. His young wife languishes for years, neglecting her children and herself in despair. One child dies, and the other is taken away to work. The hopeless woman simply sits outside her home— which grows shabbier and shabbier as time passes—as she grows weaker. Finally, inevitably, the woman dies. Perhaps in writing this poem, Wordsworth was showing some sympathy for the abandoned Annette Vallon.

This was the poem that Wordsworth read to Coleridge when he showed up at Racedown in June 1797. Wordsworth was apparently not satisfied with the poem, though. He did not try to have it published, but later reworked it into another form.

While Wordsworth wrote away, he and Dorothy also had visitors. The Pinney brothers came various times. So, too, did young Basil's father. The visitor who stayed longest was Mary Hutchinson, their old friend from childhood, just after spending many months caring for a dying sister. She came to Racedown Lodge for a rest from the strain and stayed a happy six months. It was a foreshadowing of future living arrangements.

FINDING HIS VOICE

By the late 1790s, Wordsworth was in his late twenties and his life was coming together. He had survived the deaths of both parents, the breakup of his family, and long separations from his dear sister Dorothy. He had weathered tense relations with his uncles. After some uncertainty over what career he would follow, he seemed set on the course of making his living as a poet. Later he wrote that he had decided to be a poet when he was in his teens—when he was at college and just after, however, this hardly seemed a determined course. Raisley Calvert's generosity had given him at least some money, though not quite enough for he and Dorothy to live on. Wordsworth had had two volumes of poetry published. Though they had not sold well, they had attracted the attention of people he admired, like Coleridge. He had worked hard at Racedown on two ambitious long poems and a drama. In these works he had wrestled with his feelings about the recent political and social upheavals. These, too, were praised by Coleridge and other friends whose judgment he respected.

By the time of Coleridge's 1797 visit to Racedown, then, Wordsworth was coming into his own. Most scholars judge the next ten years to be his most productive as a writer. In this time, he produced a large body of work—including most of his best poetry. A key to this success was finding his own voice. Coleridge was instrumental in that process, his influence felt from the visit of 1797.

In the summer of 1797, Wordsworth and Dorothy moved to the house at Alfoxden. It was a large, comfortable house with nine bedrooms and "furniture enough for a dozen families like ours," Dorothy wrote. In front of the house were hills topped by trees and populated by sheep and deer. Behind it, just a mile and half away, was the open water of the Bristol Channel, and nearby a stream with a delightful waterfall. There were plenty of good walks, always important to the Wordsworths. Coleridge, of course, joined in many of these walks, as did many friends who came to visit.

One of those walks led west over the Exmoor Hills along the Bristol Channel. It was November, and the air was brisk. Soon after, Coleridge began to work on his most famous poem, "The Rime of the Ancient Mariner." It tells of a seaman who suffers all his life as punishment for a crime. Wordsworth made some important contributions to the poem, including the idea of basing this suffering on a crime. While Coleridge worked on the poem, William and Dorothy went to London. They hoped to persuade a theater owner to stage *The Borderers*. They returned to Alfoxden in January, dejected over the rejections they had received.

Meanwhile, Coleridge had received some good news. He was always strapped for money, especially with a wife and child to support and another child on the way, and was considering a position as a clergyman because of the guaranteed income. At the critical moment, the poets' friend Tom Wedgwood—heir to a pottery-making company—offered to support Coleridge with £150 a year for Coleridge and his family to live on. Wordsworth, still not quite financially secure, was a bit jealous over his friend's good fortune.

In the next few months, Coleridge worked on his "Ancient Mariner" and Wordsworth continued reworking "The Ruined Cottage." Both consulted frequently with each other, giving advice and encouragement all the while. As they worked, they also talked about new projects.

What emerged became one of the most famous volumes of English poetry and the benchmark work of Romanticism, *Lyrical Ballads and Other Poems*. Most of the poems were ballads—rhyming poems that narrated a story similar to traditional folk ballads. But these were *literary* ballads, written by skillful poets, not composed over time as folk poems are. The form had recently become popular through the work of Robert Burns and others. The two young poets hoped to capitalize on this appeal and make some money by publishing some of their own. Later, they claimed that the volume reflected a plan to produce a new kind of poetry, one that found beauty in the common language of common people. While these were ideas they discussed at the time, the volume was not really planned. These ideas became the capstones of the Romantic movement. But, it would be more correct to say that the original *Lyrical Ballads* overflowed from their active minds—and it did so very quickly.

Coleridge contributed "Ancient Mariner" and three other poems, while Wordsworth filled the bulk of the volume, writing nineteen poems. A dozen of these were composed in an amazingly productive period from March to May 1798. In this time, he churned out almost 1,500 lines of poetry—even though he had only written two ballads ever before. He based the poems on stories from books that he had read or that he had heard from Dorothy or from friends, turning raw material into a dazzling array of poems.

After May he wrote the remaining poems for the book. The most notable was the one that appeared last in the volume. The full title is "Lines Composed a Few Miles Above Tintern Abbey," but it is most often simply called "Tintern Abbey." The work is unlike the other poems in the volume; it is not a ballad or a lyric but the kind of serious blank-verse poetry that Wordsworth always wanted to write. Like many of his works, it originated in a walk: a visit to the ruins of Tintern Abbey, a former monastery in southern Wales. Wordsworth later said that he composed its nearly 160 lines in his head over the course of a few days before writing any of it down.

The poem is Wordsworth's meditation on what nature was coming to mean to him. He considers how his responses to nature had changed from his childhood to the present. He declares that "nature and the language of the sense" are "The anchor of my purest thoughts, the nurse, / The guide, the guardian of my heart, and soul / Of all my moral being." In closing, he says that nature could protect him and Dorothy from the evils of human society—"rash judgments," "the sneers of selfish men," and "the dreary intercourse of daily life." Nature, he says, teaches that "all which we behold / Is full of blessings."

Literary Ballads finally came out late in 1798, published anonymously at the authors' suggestion. Coleridge still had a reputation as a political radical, which could hurt sales, while Wordsworth did not have enough of a reputation. As Coleridge put it, "Wordsworth's name is nothing—to a large number of persons mine stinks."

The reception to the volume was mixed. William Hazlitt, later an important critic, was very enthusiastic upon hearing some of the poems, which Coleridge read to him. Hazlitt wrote that he felt "the sense of a new style and a new spirit in poetry," and had the same feeling "that arises from the turning up of fresh soil, or of the first welcome breath of spring." Most critics were less kind. One of the harshest reviews came from Coleridge's one-time friend Robert Southey, who would become poet laureate of England. Still, the book became popular enough to call for a second edition just two years later. And the book's initial lack of acceptance is now largely irrelevant. The publication of *Lyrical Ballads* is now seen as a breakthrough for English poetry.

The poets, however, were not in England to see the harsh reviews. They had left the country to follow up on Coleridge's next bright idea. He convinced Wordsworth and Dorothy to go to Germany, where he wanted to learn more about the new philosophy and the language. The need to raise money for the trip was what spurred Wordsworth to write so many poems for *Literary Ballads*.

Both William and Dorothy suffered seasickness while crossing the English Channel, and once they reached the city of Hamburg, they found the German people not entirely pleasant. Wordsworth once complained about the price of bread he was holding. The baker knocked the load onto the floor and kept the money. And many people avoided the Wordsworths, suspicious of their morals. The reason was due to a misunderstanding—Germans often used the word "sister" to refer to a man's mistress.

The initial plan called for them to stay in Germany for two years, studying German and philosophy, but the grand scheme wilted in reality. Soon after arriving, Wordsworth and Coleridge decided to split up. Coleridge went to Göttingen to study language at the university, and Wordsworth and Dorothy went to the small town of Goslar in the Harz Mountains. Any hopes they might have had of hiking through the mountains were dashed by the weather. They suffered through five of the coldest months in many decades. Their rooms were so cold, they needed to wear coats to move from one room to another.

Despite these hardships, Wordsworth put his time to good use. He worked on his poetry, spending most of his time on three separate projects. One was to begin writing about his youth, a project encouraged by Coleridge; he wrote much of what became the beginning of his lengthy autobiographical poem, *The Prelude*. The second was a set of lyrics called the Lucy poems. Included in this group are "Strange Fits of Passion Have I Known," "She Dwelt among the Untrodden Ways," "Three Years She Grew in Sun and Shower," and "A Slumber Did My Spirit Steal." The four Lucy poems reflect a poet's thoughts on the death of a woman he loved. The third project was the two Matthew poems, which are also about loss. The first, "The Two April Mornings," is a ballad in which an old village schoolmaster remembers the death of his little daughter. In the second, "The Fountain," the schoolmaster regrets having no children. When one of his students offers to be his son, the old man says, "Alas! that cannot be."

Though he was productive, Wordsworth and Dorothy were unhappy in Germany. Worse, they were running out of money. In April of 1799, they returned to England and spent most of the rest of the year living with Mary Hutchinson and her two brothers and sisters. In the fall, Wordsworth took Coleridge—by now also back in England—on a three-week tour of the Lake District. He showed his friend the various spots that had helped form his mind and spirit. This tour spurred him to settle with Dorothy at a cottage near Grasmere, one of the lakes in the area. They moved into the little home in late December. Though it did not have the name at the time, it is now famous as Dove Cottage.

All during 1799, Wordsworth had fretted about money and tried to find out how *Lyrical Ballads* was selling. Some more favorable reviews of the volume came out during 1799, and supplies of the book began to dwindle. Wordsworth began to work on a new edition. It would include the Lucy and Matthew poems he had written in Germany, as well as many poems that he wrote at Grasmere in another burst of creative energy. Most of these poems were about the lives of country people.

The second edition of *Lyrical Ballads* was published in January 1801. The publisher insisted on the title *Lyrical Ballads*, even though Wordsworth objected to it. His reason was simple: few of the poems in the new work fit that form. But the publisher wanted the continuity of the same title. This time, the volumes carried an author's name—but only one. Wordsworth's name appeared, but not Coleridge's. While Coleridge did not contribute any new poems to the new edition, the move certainly seemed an affront to the the other half of the original project.

Still, Wordsworth did provide the vast majority of the poems. Indeed, his impact on the volume was even greater. He watched intensely over the new book throughout the stages of setting type and proofreading. He made constant corrections to the poems and issued many instructions to the publisher on how he wanted things to look on the page. As late as December of 1800, just before publication, he was still making changes.

One other addition that Wordsworth made was a preface explaining the theory of poetry that the poems were supposed to represent. This treatise lays out the elements of an entirely new movement in poetry, Romanticism, and remains most important writing on the emerging period. Wordsworth aimed, he said, to "choose incidents and situations from common life" for his poems. This rebelled against the tradition that the most serious works, such as epics and tragedies, could only portray kings and nobles. He also said his aim was to fill his poems with the "language really used by men." Earlier poetry relied on a higher-sounding language, one that aimed to add nobility to the poetry. Wordsworth argued that the emotions of the characters in his poems make the events in them significant, not the other way around. In traditional epic or tragic poetry, grand events take place as kings wrestle with the fates of their kingdoms or struggle with their passions. Because society depends on these leaders, the reader pays attention. Wordsworth's focus was on the common life. His aims was to show that the triumphs and tragedies of ordinary people are just as powerful emotionally—not only for them, but for readers—as are those of kings. With these ideas, Wordsworth brought his republican political ideals of equality to his poetry.

And Wordsworth argued that poetry did not emerge from an objective but subjective view of the world around him. "All good poetry is the spontaneous overflow of powerful feelings," he stated. "It takes its origin from emotion recollected in tranquillity." Wordsworth's use of writing from the powerful memory of emotion is one of the main tenets in early Romanticism. This technique is most powerfully seen in his long autobiographical poem, *The Prelude*.

Critics have argued for years over whether the poems in *Lyrical Ballads* actually met the stated goals of the new poetic movement. Regardless of whether they did or not, the new volume sold well. In just six months all the copies were gone, and the publisher asked Wordsworth to prepare a new edition.

While the new volume was enjoying this success, Wordsworth was turning to an important project. Back in 1798, Coleridge had suggested that Wordsworth write an epic-length poem about man, nature, and philosophy, which Wordsworth came to call *The Recluse*. Coleridge had great hopes for the work. "I prophesy immortality to his *Recluse*," he wrote one friend. It will be "the first [and] finest Philosophical poem," he added. Wordsworth had turned to this project from time to time in the ensuing years. Gradually, he conceived it as having three parts. Only the second part, called *The Excursion*, was ever finished, however. In 1800, he wrote a portion of the first part. This poem, "Home at Grasmere," expressed his feelings about coming back to the Lake District.

What did take shape, though, was the poem that came to be called *The Prelude*, which Wordsworth had began composing while he and Dorothy were in Germany. He completed the first version by 1805, and over the course of the rest of his life, he frequently returned to it. He made many changes over time, but never prepared it for publication. It was published by his wife after his death.

She gave it the name *The Prelude, or the Growth of the Poet's Mind*. The title correctly summed up how Wordsworth saw the poem in relation to *The Recluse* and how he saw its purpose: Wordsworth aimed *The Prelude* as a kind of preface or introduction to *The Recluse*. As an autobiography, it explained what had influenced him and shaped his thinking. The goal, in a sense, was to establish his authority for the views that would come in the longer poem.

NEW TRIALS

Sometime in 1800 or 1801, Wordsworth began to think of marriage. The object of his affections was Mary Hutchinson, the childhood friend with whom he and Dorothy had stayed in touch. A letter to her from the spring of 1801 suggests that his feelings toward her had grown quite strong. Wordsworth did not feel that he could marry immediately, however, because he felt that his affair with Annette Vallon left him under an obligation. They had corresponded over the years, although getting letters through was difficult with the war. But as long as England and France were at war, he could not see her.

Such a visit became possible early in 1802 when the two countries signed a peace agreement. Wordsworth and Dorothy made arrangements to make the journey and meet with Vallon and his daughter in the port city of Calais. They stayed a month.

Unfortunately, there are no records revealing the details of what must have been an emotionally difficult month. Dorothy's journal, usually informative, has only two pages on their stay in Calais. Those lines speak of walks on the beach and not what was said. William wrote no poems about the experience, nor did he refer to it in *The Prelude*. Clearly, though, Wordsworth informed Vallon she could have no hopes of marrying him.

Fortunately, Wordsworth and Vallon apparently left on amicable terms, and they kept in contact over the remaining years. Once he was more comfortable, Wordsworth provided a sum of money to Caroline each year—a decision that Mary Hutchinson knew about and approved of. And 18 years later, Mary and Annette met when the Wordsworths toured France. They also saw Caroline, then a married woman with children of her own.

The 1802 visit over, the Vallons headed back to Blois and the Wordsworths to England. The poet did produce some poems based on this short trip, but they were political and not personal. His sonnets about France worry about the character of the new French leader, Napoleon Bonaparte, while the poems about England reflect his joy at seeing welcome sights of home and a relief that this country would not suffer a Bonaparte. "Thou art free, / My Country!" he exalted. These poems use the form called the sonnet.

1802 was a year of resolution for Wordsworth. Annette Vallon had been a nagging issue for Wordsworth for years, and the trip to France settled their relationship for good. Another longstanding situation was resolved in 1802. Lord Lowther, the former employer of Wordsworth's father, died in May. When he died, the Wordsworth children's claim for the money he owed their father was still not settled, but his heir soon indicated he was willing to cover the debt. Richard Wordsworth, the lawyer brother, promptly sent a bill for nearly £10,400—more than half of which was 20 years worth of interest. William objected to his brother's insistence on interest, fearing that the new lord would balk at paying the extra money. In tight financial conditions, he preferred having some money rather than none. Another death later in the year reminded him that he had few other prospects for money. Uncle John Robinson died and left some money to brothers Christopher and John, but he left nothing to William. Apparently the old politician was still angry that he had not applied himself more diligently in college. Eventually the new Lord Lowther agreed to pay £8,000. It was paid out early in 1803 and divided among the children.

With the Vallon issue settled, Wordsworth and Mary were free to wed. While the event brought them joy, it was difficult emotionally for others. Wordsworth's brother John, now a sea captain, had also wished to marry Mary. When she wrote him of her decision to chose William, he replied sorrowfully, "I have been reading your letter over [and] over again my dearest Mary till tears have come to my eyes." He concluded that he would love her "to the last."

Dorothy, too, had to recognize that her relationship with her brother would change. They had lived alone together—though often with guests—since 1795. That would no longer be the case. All had agreed that she would continue to live with William and Mary, but the situation would be different. Mary would now be mistress of the house, and Dorothy would simply be an add-on. She loved Mary Hutchinson, and the two got along very well, but the marriage was a strain for her. She was so overcome with emotion that she was unable to attend the ceremony.

The new pattern of the Wordsworths' lives was quickly set, though. A wedding breakfast followed the early morning ceremony. Then William, Mary, and Dorothy left for the cottage at Grasmere that would become home to all three.

It is easy to see why Dorothy got along so well with Mary Wordsworth. She was, of course, a lifelong friend. She was also generous, as her kindness to Caroline Wordsworth showed. She did not have the talent of Dorothy, whose journals use powerful language to describe scenery and events. Indeed, one contemporary author once dismissed her as being "weak intellectually beyond the normal standards of female weakness." But she was a strong person. Living with as dedicated a writer—and as much an egotist—as Wordsworth would demand strength in a spouse, the relationship of husband and wife grew stronger over the years. In a letter written to her many years later, Wordsworth proclaimed his deep love for his wife: "I love thee so deeply and tenderly and constantly, and with such perfect satisfaction delight & happiness to my soul, that I scarcely can bring my pen to write of any thing else." Finally, Mary was a help to Wordsworth in his work. As Dorothy had done—and still continued to do—she copied drafts of poems into notebooks, creating fair copies that he could revise again. And she helped by putting up with his travels, his long hours of work, and his need for encouragement.

They had five children. John was born in 1803, Dorothy (called Dora) in 1804, Thomas in 1806, Catherine in 1808, and William in 1810. When Wordsworth's sister Dorothy became ill in the 1830s, daughter Dora became his frequent walking companion. At times in these walks, they were joined by Coleridge's first son Hartley, who lived nearby. The trio walking down a path was an echo of the earlier jaunts Wordsworth had enjoyed with his sister and his friend.

The life changes brought about by Wordsworth's marriage did not alter everything. Just two months after John was born, Wordsworth and Dorothy took a trip to Scotland, stopping for Coleridge on the way. Mary was left alone with her first child, as Coleridge's wife was left alone with their three. Coleridge was having greater success than ever before as an essayist. But he suffered from poor health and had difficulty writing poetry. The Wordsworths hoped to revive his spirits. Unfortunately, the trip could not achieve that. Instead, the close quarters created irritations and petty annoyances that made the old friends squabble and bicker.

The trio stopped at the grave of Robert Burns, the poet who had been celebrated as Scotland's national poet until his death in 1796. Wordsworth did not approve of the poet's loose lifestyle, but he had long admired Burns for his original language. Soon after that visit, rainy weather set in and followed the travelers day after day. They were riding in an open carriage, vulnerable to the rain and wind. Coleridge, annoyed by the weather, fed up with the arguments, and tormented by sleepless nights, decided to separate from the Wordsworths. The following spring, he left England for the warmer climate of Malta in the Mediterranean Sea. He hoped to find better health there and remained for more than a year.

William and Dorothy continued on their Scotland trip alone, stopping to meet Walter Scott, another masterful writer. Scott was a year younger than Wordsworth and writing the poetry that made him famous—not the historical novels for which he is most known today. He had collected and edited many folk ballads of Scotland in a volume called *Minstrelsy of the Scottish Border.* Now he was at work on a long narrative poem titled *The Lay of the Last Minstrel.* He read some of the work aloud to the Wordsworths, who admired it. He and Wordsworth remained friends for the rest of their lives. Soon after the visit, William and Dorothy returned home.

Wordsworth spent much of the next two years adding to *The Prelude.* He greatly expanded the earlier version of the poem, creating a structure of twelve major divisions, called books. In this, he echoed the great epic poems like John Milton's *Paradise Lost.* In writing his own poetic autobiography, then, Wordsworth was creating a new kind of epic. His work in 1804 and 1805 brought the poem up to the return from France in 1793.

As an autobiography, *The Prelude* is not entirely reliable. Wordsworth shaped the events and feelings of his life according to how he saw them later—adhering to his belief that poetry "takes its origin from emotion recollected in tranquility." The work is not an effort to tell the truth of his life but to explain how his mind developed and how he found his calling as a poet. As a result, he chose what to reveal about his life according to whether or not it suited this purpose. He was also influenced by a new impulse: as a married man with two children, he did not wish to be as frank about every part of his past, including his affair with Annette Vallon. Hence, as critics argue, he obscured those events in the fiction about Vaudracour and Julia. To add to this, he was growing more conservative politically than he had been in his youth. As a result, he glossed over his passionate republicanism from the early 1790s.

In 1804 and 1805, Wordsworth worked quickly on *The Prelude*, writing as much as a hundred lines a day. Then, suddenly, he stopped. He had reached parts of his life—the confused years of the early 1790s— that he did not wish to discuss. Another reason was grief. Early in 1805, his brother John's ship was wrecked on its way to a trading voyage to China. John, the captain, remained with the ship until it sank. His body was not found until months later, when it washed onto the beach.

John's death was doubly tragic. First, of course, was the painful loss of a brother, a loss which hurt Wordsworth deeply. "I feel that there is something cut out of my life which cannot be restored," he wrote in a letter a month later. Given the fact that John had courted Mary, his death must have touched her deeply as well. The second loss was financial. William and Dorothy had both invested some of their money in the voyage in hopes of receiving the rich profits that John had promised. It was John's goal to earn William enough that he could live comfortably and focus on his great poem, *The Recluse*. His death was the death of that dream.

A year later, Wordsworth wrote a powerful poem expressing his grief over his brother's death. In it, he reflects the bitterness that he still felt: "The feeling of my loss will ne'er be old." Part of the healing from that loss took place at the palatial home of Sir George Beaumont, a wealthy patron of the arts. Beaumont, who met Wordsworth in 1803, so admired *Lyrical Ballads* that he bought some land for Wordsworth near his own. In 1806, he invited the whole Wordsworth family to his estate in central England.

The following year, two important events took place. For the first time, Wordsworth revealed his completed *Prelude* to another poet. Coleridge had returned to England, and Wordsworth was eagerly waiting for him so he could read him *The Prelude*. Coleridge, as he had from the start, praised Wordsworth extravagantly, calling him "Friend of the wise! and Teacher of the Good!" and labeling his massive poem a "song divine of high and passionate thoughts."

The second significant event of 1807 was the publication of *Poems, in Two Volumes*. For the first time, Wordsworth declared himself in print in a volume composed entirely by him. This was Wordsworth, pure and simple. As with the second edition of *Lyrical Ballads*, he fussed and fretted over the book, sending orders to the printer on how the poems should be placed on the page.

The volume contained a wide variety of poems, from his political sonnets to short lyrics to longer, more pensive odes. One of the odes was "Resolution and Independence," in which he praises the virtues that he thinks a great poet must possess. Another was one of Wordsworth's most famous works, the ode "Intimations of Immortality." In it, he reflects sadly on how he has lost the intimate connection with the essential nature of the world that he had as a child. He closes the poem by asserting that he can find strength in the memories of those feelings and in faith. His place as a preeminent nature poet was secured by the short lyric "I Wandered Lonely as a Cloud," in which the poet recollects with pleasure a walk that revealed spring daffodils shining golden in the sun and dancing in the breeze. But the collection also shows that Wordsworth was more than a nature poet. The sonnet "Composed upon Westminster Bridge" is a celebration of London: "Earth has not anything to show more fair."

The reviews were very harsh, however. Critics blasted the poems as "a very tedious and affected performance," "silliness," and "trash." Two criticisms in particular hit home. One writer complained that Wordsworth was too wrapped up in himself. He should, the reviewer said, "spend more time in high library and less in company with 'the moods of his own mind.'" Another said that Wordsworth erred by "connecting his most lofty, tender, or impassioned conceptions, with objects and incidents which ... readers will probably persist in thinking low, silly, or uninteresting." In other words, Wordsworth's poetry of simple country people was a waste of effort.

The reviews stung Wordsworth. He had been working on another long poem, *The White Doe of Rylstone*, similar to Walter Scott's adventurous narrative poems of the Middle Ages. The unfavorable reviews of *Poems* convinced Wordsworth to withhold his new poem from publication. He also developed a feeling of scorn toward the audience that rejected him. They were, he said in a letter, "in a state of degradation"— a harsh thing for any author to say about readers. Dorothy revealed how deeply hurt he was in one of her letters: "He has no pleasure in publishing—he even detests it—and if it were not that he is *not* over wealthy, he would leave all his works to be published after his Death."

Meanwhile, the Wordsworth family had grown to include three children with a fourth on the way. In addition, Mary's sister Sara was living with them. The small Dove Cottage was getting crowded. In May 1808, the family moved to a larger home on the other side of Grasmere. Called Allan Bank, the house was spacious enough that all the adults could now have their own bedroom—they had all been doubling up before. Those adults now included Coleridge, who had also moved in with the Wordsworths.

The new home was not a success, however. It was expensive to furnish and maintain, and the family was still struggling with money. The poor sales of *Poems, in Two Volumes* did not help. Nor did Wordsworth's refusal to try to gain some income by publishing *The White Doe*. The unhappy state of Coleridge was not helpful either. The biggest problem with the house, though, was simply that it was uncomfortable—it was windy and cold, and the chimneys did not work properly, which left the rooms constantly full of smoke. Finally, in 1811, the Wordsworths left Allan Bank for another home in Grasmere. It was the old rectory for the local church, but it was not much better.

The years from 1810 to 1812 were difficult for Wordsworth personally. One of those difficulties was the loss of his once close friend. Back in 1801, the Wordsworths, the Hutchinsons, and Coleridge had stopped on one of their walks to carve their initials on a rock. It seemed a symbol of friendship that would last forever. In less than ten years, the happy circle was broken. John Wordsworth, one of the carvers, was dead. And Coleridge and Wordsworth were about to experience a major break.

Their friendship had been fraying for years for several reasons. Coleridge was becoming more and more unstable emotionally; he had abandoned his wife and family, convinced that he was in love with Sara Hutchinson, Mary's sister. The Wordsworths viewed his behavior as foolish and a bit immoral. Worse, Coleridge was increasingly beset by pain, which he took opium and alcohol to try to alleviate. He was stricken by guilt and could not sleep because he suffered nightmares. He was somewhat jealous of Wordsworth's happy marriage and both saddened and angry over the loss of the closeness that he and Wordsworth had once enjoyed. Finally, Coleridge wanted Wordsworth to continue working on *The Recluse*, which Wordsworth seemed to be always putting it off for other projects. For his part, Wordsworth also wanted to work on the poem, but he needed Coleridge to be nearby for him to do so. He relied on the powerful overflow of ideas from Coleridge's fertile mind to fuel his work on this poem. But by this point, Coleridge's mental state and personal habits made his presence irritating.

In 1810, the growing conflict exploded. When Basil Montagu offered to take Coleridge back to London to live with him, Wordsworth warned Montagu about Coleridge's many lapses and weaknesses, including his opium addiction. In London, Montagu foolishly passed those cautions on to Coleridge. Further, he said that Wordsworth had asked him deliver this unpleasant news to Coleridge. Coleridge was outraged, blasting Wordsworth as the "bitterest calumniator" against him. He began to speak ill of Wordsworth to others in London. When Wordsworth heard of this, he did nothing. Dorothy, though, was bitterly angry at their former friend.

Soon after the rift with Coleridge, two tragedies hit the Wordsworths. Daughter Catherine, not yet four, died in June 1812. Though she had been seriously ill two years earlier, her death came as a surprise. Indeed, neither parent was home—William was in London on business, and Mary had traveled to Grasmere to visit friends. Late in the year, the remaining children all contracted measles. While the others recovered, the disease killed Thomas, the second son. His grieving parents soldiered on. Mary threw herself into nursing the other children, but she ate little and cried often. William put on a stoic front, but was deeply sorrowful. As he said in a letter, "I loved the Boy with the utmost love of which my soul is capable, and he is taken from me."

HONORED AUTHOR

In a gloomy 1813, the family could no longer bear to stay in the rectory. On top of being cold and damp, there were daily reminders of the recent tragedies. The bodies of Catherine and Thomas were buried in the cemetery that was directly across the road from the house. In 1813, they moved to a new home called Rydal Mount, south of Grasmere. It was a lovely home on a hillside overlooking the beautiful Lake Windermere. For once, the family was comfortable. The Wordsworths were to remain there for the rest of their lives.

Adding to that comfort was more financial security. Wordsworth badly needed money to support his family, along with sister Dorothy and sister-in-law Sara Hutchinson. Sales of *Poems, in Two Volumes* were very slow, and he had published nothing else. In 1812, he had written to the current Lord Lowther—son of the man his father had worked for. This was the heir who had quickly settled the claims the Wordsworth children had made against his father. Trusting in his good intentions and desperate for money, Wordsworth asked the noble for a job.

Lowther could not offer any position immediately, but he agreed to give Wordsworth £100 a year until one could be found. Two months later, he named Wordsworth as the Distributor of Stamps for Westmoreland. In effect, the poet became a tax collector. Several poets of the generation that followed criticized Wordsworth for taking the job which was, to them, a betrayal of his earlier political ideals; Wordsworth, however, was acting in the best interests of his family.

Moving to Rydal Mount and taking the government job settled two of Wordsworth's problems. Other healings were taking place as well. Just before the move had come a reconciliation with Coleridge. A mutual friend arranged for Wordsworth to send a letter to Coleridge explaining that he had never told Montagu to say anything. He might have been critical, the letter said, but he never meant to insult Coleridge. Coleridge accepted the explanation, and the quarrel ended, but the two were never as close again as they had been.

The year after the move to Rydal Mount, Wordsworth, Mary, and Sara Hutchinson took a holiday trip to Scotland. It was the first real vacation that husband and wife had enjoyed since their marriage back in 1802.

Though he was settled domestically, and reconciled with Coleridge, Wordsworth still was not satisfied. He had not published any poetry since 1807's *Poems*, and though time had passed, the critics were still berating him for that effort. In 1812, one critic wrote that Wordsworth should be "ashamed" of most of the poems in that volume. He also declared a rival poet—not Wordsworth—as "the most original writer" around.

Wordsworth was determined to convince the critics that his grand vision of himself as a poet was justified. In 1813 and 1814, he completed work on *The Excursion*. This long narrative poem was meant to be the second part of the mammoth *The Recluse*, his exploration of man, nature, and society. *The Excursion* has nine main parts, or books. The first was built on a reworked version of the earlier poem "The Ruined Cottage."

The poem as a whole is a philosophical conversation between four characters, the Poet, the Wanderer, the Solitary, and the Pastor. The poem is rather wordy—full of ideas rather than dramatic scenes or compelling writing, but it was Wordsworth's attempt to gain artistic respectability.

When he published *The Excursion* in 1815, Wordsworth added to it a long Preface. In that work, he discussed his grand plan for the three-sectioned *Recluse*, of which *The Excursion* was the second. He also included a lengthy extract from the first section. This poem, called "Home at Grasmere," was written back in 1800, when he and Dorothy were living at Dove Cottage. He offered it as "a kind of Prospectus of the design and scope of the whole Poem," meaning *The Recluse*. Wordsworth followed up *The Excursion* with two more books of poetry in 1815. One was a two-volume collection of his shorter poems written and published to that date. It included the poems from *Lyrical Ballads*, some of the shorter poems published in 1807, and more recent work. The other was his *White Doe of Rylstone*, finally issued to the public.

This flurry of poetry was a massive, impressive undertaking. Lord Francis Jeffrey, one of the country's chief literary critics, had censored Wordsworth's work as trivial. Though Coleridge had defended him as doing more serious and weighty work, the critic had dismissed the defense. He pointed out that writers can only be known by what they publish. The new volumes of 1814 and 1815 were Wordsworth's attempt to address that criticism.

Once more, though, the reviews were harsh. Critic William Hazlitt praised the poet's imagination but repeated the view that he was too self-absorbed. Other critics were less kind. Jeffrey panned *The Excursion*, opening his review with a dismissive "This will never do." The next year, he leveled his aim at *The White Doe:* "This, we think, has the merit of being the very worst poem we ever saw imprinted." The criticisms hurt Wordsworth, though he did have the complete support of his family. And there were people, such as George Beaumont and others, who believed firmly in him and his poetry. He vowed to carry on, having faith that future generations would admire him.

While still recovering from these critical blows, Wordsworth suffered a personal one. In 1816, his brother Richard died. Wordsworth had to order his brother's affairs, which were complex and took many months to resolve.

The following year, Wordsworth entered politics. This time, though, he was not supporting the liberal republican causes of his youth. Instead, he supported a candidate for Parliament who was from the conservative Tory party. Ironically, this candidate was backed by the current Lord Lowther. Wordsworth was, in a sense, carrying on his father's work. He campaigned for the candidate for months, throwing himself into the work with energy and passion. He wrote a lengthy pamphlet in which he stated his current political views, including a ringing endorsement of the need for the country to rely on the judgment, wisdom, good intentions, and leadership of nobles. This was a far cry from the radical republican who had cheered the French Revolution.

Wordsworth was once chided about this change by an old republican friend. He charged that Wordsworth was wrong in no longer supporting France. Wordsworth defended himself, saying that he still believed in the same principles. The Revolution was what had changed, he said. First it fell into the bloodbath of the Reign of Terror; then it turned into an army ready to conquer Europe; finally, it became an empire under Napoleon. "I abandoned France and her rulers when they abandoned Liberty, gave themselves up to tyranny, and endeavoured to enslave the world."

His family feared that politics distracted Wordsworth too much from his poetry, but when the election was over he began again to work earnestly. First, he published two older works. One, "Peter Bell," was from the *Lyrical Ballads* stage. It, like many of those poems, told the story of a simple farmer. The other, "The Waggoner," was from 1806 but also dealt with country people. Though the critics had blasted Wordsworth for his choice of subjects, he defiantly continued to offer such poems.

The two volumes with these poems were followed in 1820 by some newer work, a series of sonnets dedicated to the River Duddon, which flows in the western part of the Lake District. Finally, Wordsworth received high praise for his work. The reviewer in one magazine proclaimed, "to us ... he appears beyond all comparison the most truly sublime, the most touchingly pathetic, the most delightfully simple, the most profoundly philosophical, of all the poetical spirits of the age."

The same year also saw the release of a four-volume collection of all Wordsworth's poems published to date. As was typical with Wordsworth, he poured a great deal of time and energy into completely reviewing all the poems. He made some revisions, addressing the criticisms that he had received—at least those from people whose judgment he respected. Those changes included dropping a poem that a Coleridge had deemed unsuccessful.

With the publication of all this work, Wordsworth was ready for a holiday. He and Mary set off for Europe along with Dorothy and three other friends. Wordsworth had hoped to include old friend Robert Jones in this revisit of their 1790 walk to Switzerland. Howeve, Jones, now a parson—and heavier than he had been 30 years before—could not make the trip. The trip was quite different from his and Jones's earlier jaunt. It was more of an expedition than a trek. The participants carried their goods in heavy luggage, not cloths carried on their heads. And they traveled by coach, not on foot. The chief goal of the voyage was the same, though. As Dorothy wrote, "Switzerland is our end and aim."

They visited the same pass that Wordsworth and Jones had used to cross the Alps, and saw the sights he had seen years before, comparing their present appearance to what he had remembered, as he had described them in his poems. It was a sweet experience for all. The journey seemed to reaffirm that he had achieved his goal of fixing in his memory the sights and sensations of his early life. Though the experience called forth strong emotions, Wordsworth did not translate it into new poetry. He wrote a few poems about the trip to the continent, but they were unremarkable.

On the route home, the party stopped in Paris. There they met Annette Vallon, Caroline, and her husband and children. The return trip to England was a near disaster: Wordsworth, Mary, and Dorothy were caught in a shipwreck. Fortunately, the boat was sunk near the shore, and they were rescued without harm. They reached England late in 1820.

Wordsworth's next project was a collection of more than a hundred sonnets called *Ecclesiastical Sketches*. In these poems, he tried to summarize the history of Christianity in England. The main thrust was to celebrate the Church of England and the local vicars—like his friend Jones—who worked in countless parishes across the country. To Wordsworth, these clerics defended the country morally, spiritually, and intellectually. They were, he wrote, "the principal bulwark against barbarism, and the link which unites the sequestered Peasantry with the intellectual advancement of the age." As in politics, Wordsworth had traveled far from his youth. Once he was too independent a spirit to accept becoming a clergyman. Now the clergy were the strength of England.

While Wordsworth's thinking had changed, his reputation was changing as well. The critic Jeffrey had long ago lumped Wordsworth, Coleridge, and Robert Southey together as the "Lake Poets." He meant to dismiss them for being misguided enough to want to write about nature and humble people—subjects that Jeffrey did not think worthy of poetry. Many people of similar taste agreed, but a growing public was coming to embrace that work.

Sales of Wordsworth's volumes increased. More and more people began to travel to the Lake District, drawn there by the evocative lines of Wordsworth's poetry. Many came to his home at Rydal Mount. They hoped to meet him or at least to see the study where he worked. Finally, in the 1820s, he began to win the widespread recognition he had longed for. Ironically, this recognition came at a time when he actually was writing little new poetry. He and Mary led very active social lives throughout the 1820s, journeying to London where they took in the opera and museums and spending time each year at the estates of friends like the Beaumonts or with Christopher Wordsworth, now teaching at Cambridge. They entertained a steady stream of visitors at home. Hartley Coleridge commented that each year Wordsworth was "less of the Poet, and more of the respectable, talented, hospitable Country gentleman."

THE LATER YEARS

From 1820 until his death in 1850, Wordsworth published very little although he continued to write. Some of the later poems reflect the concerns of an aging man. In "Extempore Effusion upon the Death of James Hogg," he laments the deaths of several longtime friends. Some reflect the love of nature from which he drew much of his inspiration. There are still unusual works, though, such as the sonnet that laments the existence of illustrated magazines. There is also a sonnet on railways that praises new technology. But when a railway was proposed in the Lake District—one which could be used to bring the growing number of tourists to the area—he opposed it.

He did publish two new collections in these later years. The first, *Yarrow Revisited*, came out of an 1831 trip to Scotland where Wordsworth saw an ailing Walter Scott, weakened by a stroke and ready to leave for Italy in the hopes of regaining his health. Wordsworth was shaken by Scott's condition, and the tour brought back the memories of other visits to Scotland and strong feelings of the contrast between past and present. The poems in the new volume, published in 1835, reflected these bittersweet thoughts.

The other new volume came out in 1842, and contained some of his early works never before published. Included were one version of the poem on Salisbury Plain and the old verse drama *The Borderers*. Newer works included a series on sonnets discussing the death penalty and others drawn from a trip to Italy. Largely, though, his last 30 years saw little composition. He did work on revising poems, which, for Wordsworth was nearly as intense an effort as composing them in the first place. He even returned to *The Prelude* from time to time, renewing his effort to improve his life's work.

Wordsworth continued to take political positions that seemed on the surface more conservative. In the late 1820s, he opposed the Reform Bill, a major legislative effort to expand democracy in England. First, it cut down the number of members of Parliament coming from rural districts—where they were controlled by nobles like Lord Lowther. Second, it gave more seats to the growing industrial cities. Third, it also spread the right to vote to more in the middle class. Though he opposed the bill, Wordsworth was not against the spread of the right to vote. His opposition arose from two concerns: the rising power of the new manufacturing class, the rich industrialists who owned the nation's growing factories, and the fact that the rural poor were being ignored in the reform effort.

One reason that he favored nobles in the later decades of his life was that he felt they would do more to care for the poor than the new class of wealthy manufacturers would, but he did not think that aristocrats should be too exalted above others. "One would wish to see the rich mingle with the poor as much as may be upon a footing of fraternal equality," he wrote. John Stuart Mill, a liberal political thinker, felt that his positions and Wordsworth's were not that far apart. They were, he said, simply "two travellers pursuing the same course on opposite sides of the river."

Perhaps Mill based this comment on the idea that Wordsworth's heart was in the right place. The aging poet certainly enjoyed the company of wealthy nobles and even favored them politically against industrial leaders, but his heart was touched by the poor and downtrodden. He showed this in many ways where it was most important—in his daily life. One of the new friendships he struck late in life was with an Irish soldier named Edward Quillinan. He lived near Rydal with his wife and two children. He was away from home for a time in 1822 when his wife received serious burns. The Wordsworth family cared for her until she died and for the children for some time afterward. The kindness earned Quillinan's gratitude and affection. Quillinan was not the only new friend that Wordsworth made in his later years. Many of these new friends were younger people, which helped keep Wordsworth energized.

Still, as happens to most people as they age, Wordsworth also had to face the loss of friends. George Beaumont died in 1827, Walter Scott in 1832, and Charles Lamb in 1834. Saddest, perhaps, was the passing of Coleridge in 1834. Though the two poets had never regained the closeness of their early years together, their relationship did become smoother later in life. In 1828, Coleridge even joined Wordsworth and his daughter Dorothy on a trip to Holland, Belgium, and Germany. When Coleridge died, Wordsworth said to a friend that he was "the most *wonderful* man that he had ever known, wonderful for the originality of his mind [and] the power he possessed of throwing out in profusion grant central truths."

He suffered others pains as well. In 1831, Dorothy fell so ill that Wordsworth worried she would die. She recovered but was weakened; two years later, she suffered a terrible illness that gave her intestinal pain and swollen legs. She was forced to take laudanum—brandy mixed with opium—as Coleridge had done many years before, to handle the pain. After months, she recovered, but she was never the same. A great walker, she grew afraid to go outside lest she suffer a relapse.

Just two years later, Mary's sister Sara died, stricken by rheumatic fever. Wordsworth was despondent. "What a shade falls over [one's thoughts] when those friends have passed away," he wrote. While still in mourning, he and Mary had to handle Dorothy's continuing deterioration. She suffered from something similar to Alzheimer's disease, a gradual loss of memory and mental control. Dorothy lived until 1855. And the Wordsworths had their own health problems to deal with. Mary suffered from time to time from lumbago while Wordsworth was occasionally attacked by a severe inflammation of the eyelids.

Taking away some of the sting of these problems were some gratifying honors and recognitions received in these later years. All through the 1830s, his reputation had grown among a new generation of thinkers. They valued his championing of the poor and the deep spiritual feeling in his poetry. In 1839, Wordsworth was awarded an honorary degree from Oxford University and in 1843, he was named the Poet Laureate of England. This post ordinarily requires the author to produce poems on public occasions. Wordsworth felt he was too old for such work, but accepted the honor when informed that he would not be required to do any writing.

Another task of Wordsworth's later years was to try to provide for his children. While he had been able to live comfortably in the later years, he had not become wealthy. As a result, he could not provide complete security for his children. As a result, he worried about them. Those worries, at least in the case of the two boys, were compounded by problems in their character.

John, the eldest, was not a very good student. Wordsworth tried to teach him himself for some time, but that effort did not work. Eventually he was placed in another school, but he never thrived. Still, he was accepted—with his father's help—at Oxford University, and after graduation entered the clergy. Lord Lowther helped secure him his first position, at his father's request. It was ironic that the poet, who could not bear to be a clergyman himself, found such a life as desirable for his son.

William, the youngest, was more or a problem. He was rather lazy and not interested in anything. As sister Dora and a friend wrote, "he prefers sitting to standing, riding to walking, and lying in bed to anything in the world." His parents worried a great deal about his future. Even when he was in his twenties, Mary Wordsworth wrote her son letters complementing him on his penmanship and suggesting books he should read to improve his character. Despairing that he would ever make his way on his own, Wordsworth called on political friends. In 1842, he gave up the post of Distributor of Stamps in return for an annual pension that would last the rest of his life. Son William took the tax-collector's job in his place.

Daughter Dorothy, or Dora, was still more of a problem. Wordsworth loved her deeply, and she him. She was often sick and seemed to have a frail constitution, however, which increased her parents' concern over her. In the late 1830s, she became attached to

Edward Quillinan, the soldier the family had befriended. Wordsworth liked Quillinan but did not believe that he could provide adequately for his daughter. And he had no desire to lose her company. When she told him that they wanted to get married, he refused to allow it. The intercession of friends finally weakened his resolve, though it took nearly three years. Finally, in 1841, the two were wed. Wordsworth did not attend his daughter's wedding. Just as his sister Dorothy had been unable to attend his marriage to Mary, Wordsworth was too overcome to be at the church. Still, he treated Quillinan with affection and never gave up loving his daughter. She and Quillinan moved into a home near Rydal Mount.

New concerns about Dora arose just three years later, when she became extremely ill. She recovered in Portugal and returned to the Lake District in 1846. The following year, she worsened dramatically. After two months of illness, she died in May 1847. It was a terrible blow for the Wordsworths. The aging poet could not bear to walk many places near his home, for they reminded him of his daughter.

Wordsworth by now was nearing 80 years old, and he thought more and more about his own death. To leave his imprint on how people would remember him, he began dictating notes on his poems and memories of his youth. Those memories were given to a nephew, one of brother Christopher's sons. They were intended to be used as the basis of an official biography.

Two years after Dora's death, there was another loss. Hartley Coleridge died. Wordsworth had always been fond of Coleridge's son. He asked that the body be buried next to the plot where he and Mary were to be buried.

Wordsworth himself fell ill the following March after walking with Mary when the weather was wet and cold. The chill affected the old man. He suffered an attack of pleurisy, a disease of the lungs, and was forced to bed. He remained bedridden for a month, finally dying on April 13, 1850.

ASSESSING WORDSWORTH

Wordsworth helped transform English poetry. The poetry of the 1700s was formal and somewhat stiff. The values that were emphasized were balance and harmony, thought and moral values; it could be pompous and preachy. Some of these same criticisms can be leveled at

Wordsworth. Some of his long, meditative poems are too intent on teaching and provide little of the vivid language that marks exceptional poetry. Despite his claims to be writing using the language of common men, he also used formal words and phrases.

But he—along with other writers—turned poetry in a new direction. His greatest short poems use strong, sense-based, rhythmic language to convey intense feeling. Through these poems, a reader can share in the poet's experience.

Wordsworth was never quite able to create the deep philosophical poem that Coleridge had hoped he could. One reason was that he was forced into other projects to earn his living as a poet. The deeper reason, though, is that as a philosopher Wordsworth did not have the nimbleness of mind that Coleridge possessed. He could produce powerful poetry, but he could not explore all the issues that Coleridge had hoped he would. There is a third reason that *The Recluse* was never fully developed as it had been envisioned: Wordsworth poured most of his thinking into *The Prelude*. His autobiographical poem on "the growth of the poet's mind" was his real lasting achievement.

In one of his poems, Wordsworth wrote "The child is father to the man." He meant that the personality and character of an adult is shaped by the experiences of childhood. Modern psychology has made this idea a widespread one, but when Wordsworth wrote it, the idea was not widely understood. Yet this idea forms the basis of *The Prelude*, in which he traces his early life to explain how he had developed to become the poet, and the man, he was.

Wordsworth can be criticized for being self-absorbed. After all, in much of his most accomplished work he dwells on his own memories, thoughts, and feelings. While kindly and generous to others, he also made himself into the focal point of his family. But this egotism is not unusual in people of genius, artistic or otherwise, and there is no question that he loved his friends and adored his family. He had a high opinion of himself and his mission as a poet, but he also devoted himself to others. He worked to support his family, not just to glorify himself, and helped neighbors when they were in need. His political positions were not taken simply to advance his own self-interest; he tried to determine what would be beneficial for those who suffered.

Does Wordsworth's inability to create the grand philosophical poem and his egotism make him a failure? That would be a harsh judgment. While he might not have finished that grand work, he accomplished a great deal. And his works, though about him, unquestionably touched others. Philosopher John Stuart Mill grew up in England in the early 1800s, the product of a strict upbringing. In his early twenties, Mill was near a breakdown. Then, he began to read Wordsworth's poetry. He later described the effect: "What made Wordsworth's poems a medicine for my state of mind was that they expressed, not mere outward beauty, but states of feeling ... under the excitement of beauty. They seemed to be the very culture of the feelings, which I was in quest of." A famous actor of the 1800s had a similar experience. Wordsworth's poetry, he said, "made me in some respects a wiser [man], and excited in me the aspiration to become a better man." A writer can hardly ask for more than that in his life.

NEIL HEIMS

"Homely in Attire": An Introduction
to the Poetry of William Wordsworth

> *The rhymes so homely in attire*
> *With learned ears may ill agree,*
> *But chanted by your Orphan Quire*
> *Will make a touching melody.*
> —"Address to the Scholars
> of the Village School of ———"

I.

Whether at the end of the eighteenth century when most poetry spoke
with an Augustan voice reflecting lapidary elegance and aristocratic wit,
or during the twentieth century when readers had been trained to value
poetry as a self-contained linguistic event—unsentimental, elusive,
allusive, dense, symbolic and complex—the simplicity, frequent prosaism
and apparent naïveté of much of William Wordsworth's poetry can make
it difficult for many readers to appreciate much of it or to evaluate his
achievement. (His later poetry, regarded as inferior, presents, therefore,
a separate problem, but one most readers don't have to face because it is
little known and hardly read.) John Stuart Mill called Wordsworth "the
poet of unpoetical natures," not to disparage him, but to explain that
"unpoetical natures are precisely those which require poetic cultivation."
(Mill, 92) Matthew Arnold, trying to reverse the "diminution of
popularity" Wordsworth's poetry was suffering even shortly after the
poet's death in 1850, argued for the virtue of its simplicity:

The cause of its greatness is simple, and may be told quite
simply. Wordsworth's poetry is great because of the
extraordinary power with which Wordsworth feels the joy
offered to us in nature, the joy offered to us in the simple
primary affections and duties; and because of the
extraordinary power with which ... he shows us this joy, and
renders it so as to make us share it. (Arnold, 349)

Repeatedly Wordsworth attempts to show that simplicity and
profundity do not exclude each other. The profound experiences and
emotions of *Lyrical Ballads* are simple, and it is in the simple people of
those poems and in the simplicity of their lives that profundity is to be
found. Walter Pater recognized this when he characterized "the peculiar
function of Wordsworth's genius as carrying in it a power to open out
the soul of apparently little and familiar things." (Bradley, 128)

"I Wandered Lonely As A Cloud," a quintessential Wordsworth
lyric, is as available to a child as to an adult. The simplicity of its
language, the charm of its meter, the intimacy of a first person narrator,
and the visualized immediacy of its subject make it easy to enjoy and to
remember. It is a poem which can exist in the anthology of the mind
without the need of a book:

> I wandered lonely as a cloud
> That floats on high o'er vales and hills,
> When all at once I saw a crowd,
> A host, of golden daffodils;
> Beside the lake beneath the trees,
> Fluttering and dancing in the breeze.
>
> Continuous as the stars that shine
> And twinkle on the milky way,
> They stretched in never-ending line
> Along the margin of a bay:
> Ten thousand saw I at a glance,
> Tossing their heads in sprightly dance.
>
> The waves beside them danced; but they
> Out-did the sparkling waves in glee.

A bagatelle, provides significance through the speaker's reflection on how the scene gave him pleasure:

> A poet could not but be gay,
> In such a jocund company.

But there is more, although in language and thought it is as simple it is as what precedes. The last lines reveal that beyond the aesthetic pleasure of an idle moment, something even more important, in fact central to Wordsworth, is being presented: the source of the poem's power to give pleasure:

> I gazed—and gazed—but little thought
> What wealth the show to me had brought:
>
> For oft, when on my couch I lie
> In vacant or in pensive mood,
> They flash upon the inward eye
> Which is the bliss of solitude;
> And then my heart with pleasure fills,
> And dances with the daffodils.

The crux is not the encounter with the daffodils, but the re-constellation of that experience in solitude, revealing and indeed actualizing the living essence of being—both during that first encounter and in its recapitulation. That essence is produced by the interplay of perception and consciousness, which constitutes a continuing theme and subject of Wordsworth's entire body of work.

But in a poem like "Simon Lee," where the diaphanous lyricism and unfolding enjambment of "I Wandered Lonely As A Cloud" is replaced by the tramp and jingle of a ballad meter, recapitulating a touching experience can seem like an attempt to exploit and sentimentalize local color for moralistic purposes, even to the point of condescension, both to the peasant subject of the poem and to the reader. Rather than refreshing sweetness, readers may find a cloying insistence in lines like these:

> In those proud days, he little cared
> For husbandry or tillage;

To blither tasks did Simon rouse
The sleepers of the village.

....

His master's dead,—and no one now
Dwells in the Halls of Ivor;
Men, dogs, and horses, all are dead;
He is the sole survivor.

....

Few months of life has he in store
As he to you will tell,
For still, the more he works, the more
Do his weak ankles swell.
My gentle Reader, I perceive
How patiently you've waited,
And now I fear that you expect
Some tale will be related.

O Reader! Had you in your mind
Such stores as silent thought can bring,
O gentle Reader! you would find
A tale in everything.
                    ll. 14–17, 30–33, 57–68

There is no story except the story contained in the given: here is a man. That, Wordsworth wants us to know, is all the "story" we would need if we looked for the experience of communion through consciousness, rather than for narrative sensation or sensationalism.

   The naïveté and moralizing are deliberate. Wordsworth is trying to reeducate his readers as readers and as people. He knew what he was doing, trying to unsettle indifference with pathos, as he knew many readers might not. He often referred to Coleridge's dictum, "every great and original writer ... must create the taste by which he is to be relished." (Gill, 262) As sure as he was of his power as a poet and the lucidity of his verse, Wordsworth, nevertheless, did not leave it to his readers to see the essential interdependence of the seer and the seen, its significance or the significance of the poor common subjects of his poetry only from his poetry. With the second edition of *Lyrical Ballads*, in 1800, Wordworth discussed these matters in a Preface which provides a defense of his poetry and a definition of the function of poetry. "The principal object," Wordsworth writes,

> proposed in these Poems, was to choose incidents and situations from common life, and to relate or describe them throughout, as far as was possible, in a selection of language really used by men, and at the same time, to throw over them a certain colouring of imagination, whereby ordinary things should be presented to the mind in an unusual aspect; and further, and above all, to make these incidents and situations interesting by tracing in them, truly though not ostentatiously, the primary laws of our nature. (*CPW*, X.10)

"The primary laws of our nature," is not a phrase or a concept that invites us to think of simplicity, nor can "the primary laws of our nature" be readily simplified without becoming simple-minded in the reduction. It is a risk—"Simon Lee" as one of many shows—which Wordsworth repeatedly takes in his poetry. It is a teacher's gamble that his teaching can make his students worthy of it. In the Preface, Wordsworth explains that "[h]umble and rustic life was generally chosen" as the source for and subject of his poetry

> because in that condition the essential passions of the heart find better soil in which they can attain their maturity, are less under restraint, and speak a plainer and more emphatic language; because in that condition our elementary feelings co-exist in a state of greater simplicity, and, consequently, may be more accurately contemplated, and more forcibly communicated; because the manners of rural life germinate from those elementary feelings, and from the necessary character of rural occupations, are more easily comprehended, and more durable; and, lastly, because in that condition the passions of men are incorporated with the beautiful and permanent forms of nature. (*CPW*, X.10)

Similarly,

> [t]he language ... of these men has been adopted ... because such men hourly communicate with the best objects from

which the best part of language is originally derived: and because their rank in society and the sameness and narrow circle of their intercourse, being less under the influence of social vanity, they convey their feelings and notions in simple and unelaborated expressions. (*CPW*, X.10)

The purpose of poetry, Wordsworth is arguing, is to cultivate human sympathy by exciting the human mind. (*CPW*, X.10) The poet's intrusive admonition in "Simon Lee,"

> O Reader! Had you in your mind
> Such stores as silent thought can bring,
> O gentle Reader! you would find
> A tale in everything,

is not tangential but central, just as the closing verses of "I Wandered Lonely As A Cloud" are not merely an afterthought. The intrusion justifies the poem. If "Simon Lee" is successful it will bring the reader nearer to the state of having a mind stored with "silent thought." Poetry's task, Wordsworth argues in the Preface to *Lyrical Ballads*, is to develop consciousness, for consciousness shapes the meaning of the material world. The quality and intensity of consciousness depend upon the sensitivity and receptivity of the mind, whose constitution is the poet's work. For Wordsworth, the

> .... mind
> Even as the agent of one great mind,
> Creates, creator and receiver both,
> Working but in alliance with the works
> Which it beholds
> > *The Prelude* II. 271 ff.[1]

Consciousness, Wordsworth is saying, is as much *determined by* what is as it determines the *nature of* what is, whether personal, spiritual, aesthetic, social or political, all important categories to him. The story of Simon Lee must expand our humanity, and our wiser humanity finds depth and meaning in "Simon Lee." Simon Lee thus exists as defined not only by his action but by our perception of him and his action. In

Wordsworthian terms, it is essential for us to see with a loving kindness, with a heart made wise, because its influence extends and shapes the fabric of existence and of consciousness, alleviating, even reconfiguring, natural suffering and countering social injustice—accomplishing both is a primary concern of his poetry. For Wordsworth, the phenomenology of individual perception is the foundation of social behavior and political vision:

> The external world is fitted to the Mind;
> And the creation ...
> ... they with blended might
> Accomplish. (Gill, 303)

"This," Wordsworth explains, echoing Milton, "is our high argument." (Gill, 303) Rather than justifying the ways of God to Man, Milton's high argument in *Paradise Lost*, Wordsworth varies it, teaching that the given Creation is not a finished creation, but an element of the Creation, which is brought nearer completion when it is processed through the Mind. Consequently, we play a formative role in determining the nature of the Creation.

What may cause difficulty for readers is that Wordsworth is uncompromising. In "The Old Cumberland Beggar," Wordsworth not only makes an old, palsied wandering beggar his theme, but celebrates his condition for the good it does to the poor folks who give him what little charity they can. "[D]eem not this man useless," Wordsworth apostrophizes, almost scolding:

> .... ye proud,
> Heart-swoln, while in your pride ye contemplate
> Your talents, power, or wisdom, deem him not
> A burthen to the earth! 'Tis Nature's law
> That none, the meanest of created things,
> Or forms created the most vile and brute,
> The dullest or most noxious, should exist
> Divorced from good ....
> .... While from door to door,
> This old man creeps, the villagers in him
> Behold a record which together binds

Past deeds and offices of charity,
Else unremembered, and so keeps alive
The kindly mood in hearts which lapse of years,
And that half-wisdom half-experience gives,
Make slow to feel, and by sure steps resign
To selfishness and cold oblivious cares.
                    ll. 70–77, 87–95

The beggar has the same effect on the villagers that the field of daffodils
has on the poet and that Wordsworth intends his poetry to have on its
readers. A loving perception of a profound event opens them—and us
who read—to the intensity of full-experience rather the "half-
experience" Wordsworth decries. This "half-experience" is cold
knowledge, divorced from imagination, the faculty which yokes the
knower to the known, and it prevents us from understanding that we and
Nature are a unity, that we are

Rolled round in earth's diurnal course
With rocks and stones and trees.
            "A Slumber Did My Spirit Seal," ll.8–9

In order to develop this sensibility in his readers Wordsworth seems to
go to an uncompromising extreme of naïveté—risking, even courting,
the ridicule bred by the disdain sophistication can provoke—so that he
may expose the essence underneath the ridicule. By exposing and then
burning ridicule off, as if it were an obscuring fog, he hopes to release
pent-up sympathies and restore humanity.

II.

Wordsworth's greatness, according to Thomas McFarland, was
"uniquely dependent not upon poetic art but upon an originary intensity
of feeling." (McFarland, 96) Wordsworth himself asserts that "all good
poetry is the spontaneous overflow of powerful feelings" in

a man who, being possessed of more than usual organic
sensibility, [has] also thought long and deeply. For our
continued influxes of feeling are modified and directed by

our thoughts, which are indeed the representatives of all our past feelings. (*CPW*, X.9)

Poetry, therefore, for Wordsworth, is not a vehicle for emotional expression or for creating an emotional response but a discipline for releasing and revealing feeling in order to develop the sort of intellectual sensibility which refines the nature and quality of our emotional responses. He amplifies his definition of poetry later in the Preface adding,

> I have said that poetry is the spontaneous overflow of powerful feelings; it takes its origin from emotion recollected in tranquillity; the emotion is contemplated till, by a species of re-action, the tranquillity gradually disappears, and an emotion, kindred to that which was before the subject of contemplation, is gradually produced, and does itself actually exist in the mind. (*CPW*, X.31)

Wordsworth is making two points. First, he is describing the reciprocal process of mental sympathy with the environment, which shows how perceiver and perceived define and reflect each other. And he is talking about a process which combines inner awareness, retrospection and introspection. These sensitivities or skills, which for Wordsworth are at the heart of a poet, make him a fit agent for the task of poetry, whose object, he writes, "is truth, not individual and local, but general and operative; not standing upon external testimony, but carried alive into the heart by passion." (*CPW*, X.20) The poet's influence must create in readers the kind of sensibility which enabled him in the first instance to perceive the event which generated his poetry and then to compose his experience so "that the understanding of the Reader must necessarily be in some degree enlightened, and his affection strengthened and purified." (*CPW*, 9–10) For this to happen, an intensity of intelligent sympathy and unhindered attention is required. Affection is a matter of understanding, and according to Wordsworth, the poet can further both. "The human mind," Wordsworth believes,

> is capable of being excited without the application of gross and violent stimulants.... [O]ne being is elevated above

another in proportion as he possesses this capability ... that to endeavor to produce or enlarge this capability is one of the best services in which ... a Writer can be engaged. (*CPW*, 10)

For Wordsworth, as for Shelley, the poet is the legislator, not one who makes laws, but one who discovers and sets down the Laws of Nature, and guides us by his poetry to a subtle sensitivity which allows us to know and conform ourselves to those laws. The poet develops our sensitivity to perceive delicate stimuli with subtlety, and cultivates our capacity to perceive and to reflect what has been perceived by the poet's faculties. In this way, the poet exerts an influence upon our "understanding" and thereby upon the quality of our "affection." "Understanding" refers to both the ability to absorb particular events or situations and the faculty or organ of understanding itself, a faculty determined by the qualities of perception and consciousness. By means of understanding, Wordsworth believes, we perceive the unity of creation. This faculty dims as we grow older. By binding together perception and perceiver, Wordsworth sought to retrieve and restore this vision. Experiencing the unity of the world of Nature and of consciousness not only indicates the organic connection of all things in Nature but also suggests to Wordsworth the soul's immortality.

Wordsworth derives the immortality of the soul from his sense of the child's relation and response to its environment. In "Ode: Intimations of Immortality from Recollections of Early Childhood," he describes the state of childhood in terms of the child's relation to the natural world. The child experiences itself and the world as a unity.

> There was a time when meadow, grove, and stream,
> The earth, and every common sight,
>   To me did seem
>   Apparelled in celestial light,
> The glory and the freshness of a dream
> ll. 1–5

In prefatory notes later appended to the "Ode," Wordsworth wrote, "I was often unable to think of external things as having external existence, and I communed with all that I saw as something not apart from, but inherent in, my own immaterial nature." (*CPW*, V.52) He goes on to explain that he regarded "that dream-like vividness and splendour which invest objects of sight in childhood ... as presumptive evidence of a prior state of existence." (*CPW* V.53) In this, he is following Plato who, in Socrates' well-known second speech on love in the *Phaedrus*, explains attraction between two people to be the result of a memory of their association in a pre-existent dimension when they followed in the train of the same god. The child, thus, in the Platonic lore, comes into the temporal world from a previous immortal existence. Wordsworth writes:

> Our birth is but a sleep and a forgetting:
> The Soul that rises with us, our life's Star,
>   Hath had elsewhere its setting,
>   And cometh from afar.
>
> ll. 59–62

At birth, it still has memory and knowledge of the Oneness from which it has come, but as we age and grow more distant from our origin, our knowledge of this eternal Unity fades. Wordsworth writes:

> Heaven lies about us in our infancy!
> Shades of the prison-house begin to close
>   Upon the growing Boy
>   ll. 67–69

who nevertheless

> ....still is Nature's Priest.
> And by the vision splendid
> Is on his way attended
>   ll. 73–75

until

> At length the Man perceives it die away,
> And fade into the light of common day,
>   ll. 76–77

and the loss becomes complete:

It is not now as it hath been of yore; —
    Turn wheresoe'r I may
      By night or day,
The things which I have seen I now can see no more.
          ll. 6–9

This is the condition of "half-experience" which Wordsworth deplores in "Simon Lee." His poetry strives to mend it by the lesson of the inward flashing of the daffodils or the insight that the old Cumberland beggar serves the villagers by being the catalyst which activates their generosity.

The intensity of childhood experience gives memory the importance it has in Wordsworth's poetry, for by recollection we can regain a glimmer of what with childhood's passing we lost. Visions of nature can prod our memory. But the recognition in another person of what our previous connection was like can also bring the intensity of childhood experience back to us. In "Lines Composed a Few Miles above Tintern Abbey" Wordsworth reflects how his sister's enjoyment of the scene restores to him the sense of what his had been.

    .... in thy voice [he says] I catch
The language of my former heart, and read
My former pleasures in the shooting lights
Of thy wild eyes. Oh! Yet a little while
May I behold in thee what I was once.
          ll. 116–120

Beholding in her what he once was, even though he has moved away from it, keeps alive in him some of the power of sympathy he ascribes to the child and, therefore, links him with the oneness of creation and with eternity. By bringing his sister to the landscape to which he had been once so intensely drawn, moreover, and by presiding over her experience of it—sharing hers and experiencing a new one of his own—the poet assumes the vatic powers to pray and to guide that Wordsworth repeatedly asserts in his poetry:

    .... and this prayer I make,
Knowing that Nature never did betray
The heart that loved her; 'tis her privilege

Through all the years of this our life, to lead
From joy to joy: for she can so inform
The mind that is within us, so impress
With quietness and beauty, and so feed
With lofty thoughts, that neither evil tongues,
Rash judgements, nor the sneers of selfish men,
Nor greetings where no kindness is nor all
The dreary intercourse of daily life,
Shall e'er prevail against us, or disturb
Our cheerful faith, that all that we behold
Is full of blessings.

ll. 121–134

It is not only his sister's rapture that has the power to recall him to a former self nearer to the ideal unity with Nature. So does the landscape. What he has suggested in poems like "Daffodils," Wordsworth presents explicitly in poems like "Tintern Abbey," the "Intimations Ode" and "The Ruined Cottage." The landscape is as vital as the people in it. In fact, they vitalize each other and depend on each other for completeness. In "The Ruined Cottage," the aged traveler, "[t]he venerable Armytage, a friend/ As dear to me as is the setting sun," explains

..........poets, in their elegies and songs
Lamenting the departed, call the groves,
They call upon the hills and streams to mourn,
And senseless rocks—nor idly, for they speak
In these their invocations with a voice
Obedient to the strong creative power
Of human passion. Sympathies there are
More tranquil, yet perhaps of kindred birth,
That steal upon the meditative mind
And grow with thought. Beside yon spring I stood,
And eyed its waters till we seemed to feel
One sadness, they and I. For them a bond
Of brotherhood is broken: time has been
When every day the touch of human hand
Disturbed their stillness, and they ministered

To human comfort.
                          ll.73–88

Rather than composing an argument for the pathetic fallacy, Wordsworth here asserts an animism in nature dependent upon the imaginative power of a mind sympathetically tuned to the functions of nature. John Stuart Mill, not one to condone mysticism, defends Wordsworth's vision, arguing

> that the imaginative emotion which an idea, when vividly conceived, excites in us, is not an illusion but a fact, as real as any of the other qualities of objects: and far from implying anything erroneous or delusive in our mental apprehension of the object, is quite consistent with our most accurate knowledge and most perfect practical recognition of all its physical and intellectual laws and relations. (Mill, 93)

III.

Wordsworth complained that the circumstances of late eighteenth-century life hindered the development of the capacity for imaginative reciprocity between person and nature. The mental excitement he deemed necessary for cultivating the mind's power was an excitement derived from the subtle and delicate opportunity for quiet communion tranquilly realized through perception of natural phenomena. Following upon this intercourse, a passionate disturbance, resulting from it, ensues, and calls up spontaneous and heightened emotions, which, in their realization in language, become poetry. Wordsworth lamented however that:

> A multitude of causes, unknown to former times, are now acting with a combined force to blunt the discriminating powers of the mind, and, unfitting it for all voluntary exertion, to reduce it to a state of almost savage torpor. The most effective of these causes are the great national events which are daily taking place, and the increasing accumulation of men in cities, where the uniformity of their occupations produces a craving for extraordinary incident which the rapid

> communication of intelligence hourly gratifies. To this tendency of life and manners the literature and theatrical exhibitions of the country have conformed themselves. The invaluable works of our elder writers ... are driven into neglect by frantic novels, sickly and stupid German Tragedies, and deluges of idle and extravagant stories in verse. (*CPW*, X.10–11)

During the decade before he wrote these words for the 1800 Preface to *Lyrical Ballads*, Wordsworth had himself been stirred by "a multitude of causes." His ballad "Strange Passions Did My Spirit Seal" shows the influence of the gothic lyricism of Goethe's *Erlkoenig*, even to the identity of the breath-stopping last word of both—"dead." "National events daily taking place" in France absorbed and involved him. It was the moment of the great and then terrible revolution there, and the era of its influence.

The last thirty years of the eighteenth-century represented a period of immense turmoil, transition and redefinition in human history. Previously unquestioned institutions and practices as well as massive social structures were challenged, destroyed, and replaced. So was the definition of the person and of individual worth. The same year as Wordsworth was born, in 1770, the literary movement in Germany called *Sturm und Drang*—in English, "Storm and Stress"—began. It was inspired by the explosive social ideas of Jean-Jacques Rousseau, especially by his formulation that rightful personal liberty, inherent in each individual, was thwarted by the chains of social institutions, rules, habits and customs. Consequent upon this assertion was Rousseau's belief in an education for children which respected them as natural creatures needing to interact with the natural world and not be weaned away from it by books or schooling. Six years after Wordsworth's birth, Thomas Jefferson wrote the American Declaration of Independence in which he justified "dissolving political bands," by arguing that

> all men are created equal; that they are endowed by their Creator with certain unalienable Rights; that among these are Life, Liberty and the pursuit of Happiness; that to secure these rights, Governments are instituted among Men, deriving their just powers from the consent of the governed;

that whenever any Form of Government becomes destructive of these ends, it is the Right of the People to alter or to abolish it, and to institute new Government, laying its foundation on such principles and organizing its powers in such form, as to them shall seem most likely to effect their Safety and Happiness.

Thirteen years after that, when Wordsworth was nineteen, the French Revolution began.

A year later, in the company of his friend Richard Jones, Wordsworth set off for a walking tour of the continent. They crossed from Dover to Calais on July 13, 1790, the eve of the first anniversary of the fall of the Bastille, when the still enthroned Louis XVI "pledged his allegiance to the new constitution at an altar erected at the Champs de Mars." (Gill, 45) This excursion reveals both of the commitments that engaged Wordsworth lifelong, Nature and Justice, although his conception of them, as we shall see, altered in his later years. As they walked across France to revel in the scenic and immerse themselves in nature, Wordsworth and Jones also partook of the excitement of the new order. Wordsworth returned to England in October 1790 where repercussions from the French Revolution were being felt in the agitation for greater political and religious liberty in England. Richard Price, a Dissenting minister, proclaimed:

... now, methinks I see the ardour for liberty catching and spreading; a general amendment beginning in human affairs; the dominion of kings changed for the dominion of laws; the dominion of priests giving way to the dominion of reason and conscience. (Gill, 53)

Wordsworth himself—although his family was set upon his becoming a curate in the established Church of England—spent his time in the company of Dissenters, among them Samuel Nicholson, "a member of the Society for Constitutional Information, a pressure group for political reform." With him Wordworth attended meetings where he heard radical orators preach. (Gill, 55–56)

In November of 1791, Wordsworth returned to France. He met Annette Vallons; they became lovers; she bore a daughter whom

Wordsworth acknowledged, visited and supported throughout his life. At first, it seems he wanted to marry Annette, but lack of money and a war that made travel between England and France impossible played their part in preventing it. So did their religious differences. In Paris, Wordsworth saw firsthand the complex intermixture of the early promise and the subsequent danger of revolution, that ungoverned liberty can become tyranny. He saw power struggles, brutality and the incipient terror. In the beginning, his sympathies were with the revolution. In December 1791, he wrote to Richard Jones, "all the people of any opulence are aristocrates and all others democrates" (Mill, 60), and by September 1792, he concluded *Descriptive Sketches* crying:

> Oh give, great God, to Freedom's waves to ride
> Sublime o'er Conquest, Avarice, and Pride,
> To break, the vales where death with Famine scow'rs
> And dark Oppression builds her thick-ribb'd tow'rs:
> Where Machination her fell soul resigns,
> Fled panting to the center of her mines;
> Where Persecution decks with ghastly smiles
> Her bed, his mountains mad Ambition piles;
> Where Discord stalks, dilating every hour,
> And crouching fearful at the feet of Pow'r
> Look up for sign of havoc, Fire and Sword;
> Give them, beneath their breast while Gladness springs,
> To brood the nations o'er with Nile-like wings,
> And grant that every sceptered child of clay,
> Who cries, presumptuous, 'here their tides shall stay,'
> Swept in their anger from th'affrighted shore,
> With all his creatures sink—to rise no more.
> ll. 792–809

The poetry is good eighteenth-century bombast and much more like a Dissenter's rallying sermon than an example of emotion recollected in tranquility. It was published in England in January 1793, a month after Wordsworth returned from France and a week after Louis XVI was guillotined.

By the closing years of the decade, the revolution in France had shown that liberty unchecked and ungoverned tended toward voracity;

then the revolution of the people turned into Napoleonic imperialism; Europe was ravaged by war. England was not only in that war but had imprisoned or transported a number of men, not who had acted violently, but who had freely spoken or written for liberty and against war. (Mill, 76–77) By the closing years of the decade Wordsworth no longer supported revolution or France. Liberty became for him more of an internal than an external quality, and he found virtue in constraint, as he shows in his sonnet "Nuns Fret Not." In that sonnet—perhaps alluding to his own youthful pre-marital sexuality through the use of Claudio's expression confessing his in *Measure for Measure*—he complains of having "felt the weight of too much liberty." He saw an eternal design in human suffering, rather than a cause for revolution and upheaval. He had seen "the revolution ... rapidly advancing to its extreme of wickedness." (Erdman, 35:6) Indeed, evidence, including Wordsworth's own testimony, in an 1842 recollection, tends to indicate that Wordsworth was again in Paris in October of 1793, saw the full-blown reign of terror and guillotining, and himself narrowly escaped capture. (Erdman, 362–366) Writing later in *The Prelude* about this period and his enthusiasm, Wordsworth says:

> What then I learn'd, or think I learn'd, of truth!
> And the errors into which I was betray'd
> By present objects, and by reasonings false
> From the beginning, inasmuch as drawn
> Out of a heart which had been turn'd aside
> From Nature by external accidents,
> And which was thus confounded more and more,
> Misguiding and misguided.
> X. 882–889

Wordsworth takes this period to be an erroneous interlude, culminating in a dangerous deviation from his life with Nature, snared by the "external accidents" of history. In *The Prelude*, as well as in the "Intimations Ode," repeatedly he details the importance of Nature for his very identity, characterizing himself as formed in childhood and youth by his association with Nature:

> the fairest of all Rivers, lov'd
> To blend his murmurs with my Nurse's song,

And from his alder shades and rocky falls,
And from his fords and shallows, sent a voice
That flowed along my dreams[.] For this, didst Thou
O Derwent! Travelling over the green Plains
Near my 'sweet birthplace', didst thou, beauteous stream,
Make ceaseless music through the night and day
Which with its steady cadence, tempering
Our human waywardness, composed my thoughts
To more than infant softness, giving me,
Among the fretful dwellings of mankind,
A knowledge, a dim earnest, of the calm
That Nature breathes among the hills and groves.
.... I grew up
Foster'd alike by beauty and by fear:
Much favor'd in my birthplace, and no less
In that beloved Vale to which, erelong,
I was transplanted. Well I call to mind
...... when upon the mountain slope
the frost and breath of frosty wind had snapp'd
The last autumnal crocus, 'twas my joy
To wander half the night among the Cliffs
And the smooth Hollows, where the woodcocks ran
Along the open turf.
                    I.272–316

He returned to Nature, he writes in "Tintern Abbey,"

.... more like a man
Flying from something that he dreads than one
Who sought the thing he loved.
                    ll. 70–72

The lines were penned in 1793 when he was flying from his shattered political hope and his youthful exuberance. The democratic ideals which the French revolution betrayed, however, were not discredited ideals for Wordsworth; it was the way of their actualization, not the ideals, that had proven faulty. The revolution had unleashed the turmoil that leads to brutality rather than created the tranquility in which the individual soul can grow in natural freedom. It was to the cultivation, then, of the growth of the soul that Wordsworth dedicated his talent. He sought to write phenomenological and philosophical poetry using his own experience, his memory and his passionate analysis of memory and experience to study what it is to be human and, in Arnold's phrase, "how to live." (Arnold, 342) The energy that had been released in the excited dedication to an ideal cause now was channeled into the service of the ideal of poetry. The matters that made the French Revolution matter—poverty, injustice, desperate situations, the suffering of common people who are noble in their endurance in spite of or inside of their plight, and an expressive language drawn from common speech—became the matter of much of his poetry. (*CPW*, 117–118)[2] Moreover, a sense that spiritual unity was derived from an inward relation with external nature—its absence in France had led to terror— became a guiding principle for Wordsworth.

The influences which brought him back to his faith in Nature, and to a full sense of his identity and mission as a poet were three. The first was Nature itself as, among numerous passages, these two examples from *The Prelude* declare:

> .... if in this time
> Of dereliction and dismay, I yet
> Despair not of our nature; but retain
> A more than Roman confidence, a faith
> That fails not, in all sorrow my support,
> The blessing of my life, the gift is yours,
> Ye mountains! Thine, O Nature! Thou hast fed
> My lofty speculations; and in thee,
> For this uneasy heart of ours I find
> A never-failing principle of joy,
> And purest passion.
>   [II. 456–466].

> .... Nature's Self, by human love
> Assisted, through the weary labyrinth
> Conducted me again to open day,
> Revived the feeling of my earlier life,
> Gave me that strength and knowledge full of peace
> Enlarged, and never more to be disturb'd

Which through the steps of our degeneracy,
All degradation of this age, hath still
Upheld me, and upholds me at this day
In the catastrophe ....
.... when finally to close
And rivet up the gains of France, a Pope
Is summon'd in to crown an emperor.
                    X. 922–934

Of the two people who aided in his restoration, one was his closest friend, the poet Samuel Taylor Coleridge, who also had been excited by revolutionary hope, and then disillusioned. Coleridge spent many hours encouraging Wordsworth to formulate a visionary and philosophical epic worthy of his labor and beneficial to "mankind," as a counterbalance to the failed hope, as this excerpt from one of his letters shows:

I wish you would write a poem, in blank verse, addressed to those, who, in consequence of the complete failure of the French Revolution, have thrown up all hopes of the amelioration of mankind. (Johnson, 680)

The other was his sister, Dorothy.

William and Dorothy had been parted and had seen each other only fleetingly since 1778, when they were orphaned by the death of their mother. They were reunited in 1787 when William was seventeen and Dorothy fifteen. He gives to Dorothy the same generative power he gives to the river Derwent, representing her as a brook, when he says of her:

That belovèd Woman in whose sight
Those days were pass'd, now speaking in a voice
Of sudden admonition, like a brook
That does but cross a lonely road, and now
Seen, heard and felt, and caught at every turn,
Companion never lost through many a league,
Maintain'd for me a saving intercourse

With my true self; for, though impaired and chang'd
Much as it seemed, I was no further chang'd
Than as a clouded, not a waning moon:
She, in the midst of all, preserv'd me still
A Poet.
                    X. 909–920

                    IV.

Wordsworth has earned a place in the pantheon of English poets because
of what has come to be called his Great Decade, the years beginning
around 1797 and ending around 1806. It is generally agreed that there
followed a serious decline in his powers. In the first canto of *Don Juan*,
published in 1819, Byron repeatedly takes swipes at Wordsworth, calling
him "crazed beyond all hope," (I. ccv), and commending his own verse
by arguing that

When Southey's read and Wordsworth's understood,
I can't help putting in my claim to praise.
                    I. ccxxii

His full opprobrium comes early in the Dedication:

And Wordsworth in a rather long "Excursion,"
    (I think the quarto holds five hundred pages),
Has given a sample from the vasty version
    Of this new system to perplex the sages;
'Tis poetry—at least by his assertion,
    And may appear so when the dog-star rages—
And he who understands it would be able
To add a story to the Tower of Babel.
                    iv

At the publication of *The Excursion*, he wrote:

Wordsworth's last quarto, by the way, is bigger
    Than any since the birthday of typography;
A drowsy, frowzy poem called the "Excursion,"

Writ in a manner which is my aversion.
                    III. xciv

Shelley, whose verse could be far more raveled than any of Wordsworth's and who did not rely on a wit that might exalt at other men's follies, too, found Wordsworth's later work a matter for reproach, betraying, as it seemed to him, the wonder of his earlier poetry. After reading parts of *The Excursion*, Shelley wrote in a sonnet, "To Wordsworth,"

> Thou hast like to a rock-built refuge stood
> Above the blind and battling multitude:
> In honored poverty thy voice did weave
> Songs consecrate to truth and liberty,—
> Deserting these, thou leavest me to grieve,
> Thus having been, that thou shouldst cease to be.

Mary Shelley, pained by the conservative turn of Wordsworth's views, on the same occasion simply noted in her journal, "He is a slave." (Gill, 320) Francis Jeffrey, the influential critic of *The Edinburgh Review*, from the start found much to dislike about Wordsworth's poetry. As early as 1802, Jeffrey complained that Wordsworth's practice of using common speech in poetry indicated "splenetic and idle discontent with the existing institutions of society." (Gill, 224) He argued that Wordsworth connects "his most lofty, tender or impassioned conceptions, with objects and incidents which the greater part of his readers will probably persist in thinking low, silly, or uninteresting." (Gill, 268) In 1812, he mocked Wordsworth for writing "ecstacies about spades or sparrows' eggs—or men gathering leeches—or women in duffle cloaks—or plates and porringers—or wash tubs." (Gill, 301) His response to *The Excursion* began with disdain and dismissal, "This will never do." He scorns what he characterizes as "the mystical verbiage of the methodist puplit," and he sees Wordsworth presenting himself as "the elected organ of divine truth and persuasion." (Gill, 305) Even a friendly critic like Matthew Arnold, who had met Wordsworth and had lived nearby his home at Rydal Mount as a boy, wrote,

> ... in his seven volumes the pieces of high merit are mingled
> with a mass of pieces very inferior to them; so inferior to

them that it seems wonderful how the same poet should have produced both.... Work altogether inferior, work quite uninspired, flat and dull, is produced by him with evident unconsciousness of its defects, and he presents it to us with the same faith and seriousness as his best work. (Arnold, 338)

Geoffrey Hartman characterizes reading *The Excursion* as "a massively depressing experience," because one cannot escape "the haunting suspicion that it is a second rate work," and concludes that "[t]he betrayal of possible sublimity is impossible to forgive." (Hartman, 292) He then offers a reading of the poem that suggests far more its greatness than its failure. A.C. Bradley, a critic whose penetration cannot be dismissed, writing a century earlier says of *The Prelude* and *The Excursion*, "though there are dull pages in both, [both] contain much of Wordsworth's best and most characteristic poetry." (Bradley, 128–9)[3] Despite such significant caveats, most serious readers of Wordsworth would agree, although perhaps in less uncompromising language, with Thomas McFarland's assessment of the poetry Wordsworth composed during the latter part of his life:

The visionary splendour faded, Coleridge no longer there to spur him and guide him, rigidity in politics and religion deadening him, still he wrote. And he irritates; for it was only by the presence of his unique intensity that he was a great poet, and that intensity gone, he scarcely deserved the name of poet at all. (McFarland, 97)

"The visionary splendour faded." Why, how? McFarland suggests, echoing Arnold, the absence of Coleridge's guidance, as one reason. That may be, although it is to Coleridge's influence that Hartman suggests some of the ponderousness of *The Excursion* may be attributable, as it seeks to be the philosophical poem Coleridge urged him to write (Hartman, 316). McFarland also cites "rigidity in politics and religion deadening him." Perhaps these were effects, however, rather than causes, symptoms of a disturbance and defenses against it. About causes, it may be impossible to speak confidently, and foolish to speculate. Perhaps, however, consideration of correspondences may be suggestive even if not conclusive. They are surely formidable. A forced revision of youthful political ideals and allegiances, loosening himself from the grip of an untenable relationship with his sister, seeing Coleridge become unstable and at emotional loose ends, the demands of earning money, and the establishment of marriage and domesticity all corresponded with the onset of poetic decline and political and religious contraction.

It is possible, too, that the sensibility which made Wordsworth's greatness is the same force that allowed his weakness. The quality Wordsworth declares essential for composing poetry in the 1800 Preface is receptivity bordering on vulnerability. It invites a fertilizing penetration of the mind by a passion derived from the contemplation of something outside the self, which totally absorbs the self. It is a generative disturbance to which the poet must be sensitively attuned. This faculty of receptive vulnerability demands an innocence that finds the surrounding world receptive, as well. Otherwise, without the world returning a reciprocal receptivity, the self is threatened with a lack of grounding, with the bottomless torment of which Coleridge complains in "Work without Hope,"

> Work without Hope draws nectar in a sieve,
> And Hope without an object cannot live.

What Wordsworth learned from experience in the middle 1790s was not that his ideals and desires were errant, but that the world of Mankind, full of struggle and imperfection, did not accommodate the reciprocal receptivity he enjoyed in Nature. His response was to withdraw into himself and his domesticity, circumscribing the realm of his vulnerability within his own receptivity to stimuli lodged in his memory and his perception. As a poet he established himself as a transmitting medium for feelings and sensations which realize inner transport and ecstasy. Through poetry reflecting this condition and its products, he hoped to reintroduce mankind to nature as something fundamental and immutable, something to be relied on despite the apparent transience of pleasure or the corruptibility of ideals. In many ways he succeeded. John Stuart Mill, overwhelmed by a dread that nothing in the world was important, that even if his utopian Utilitarian goals were achieved, he could find no reason to live, found a way out of his depression reading Wordsworth and feeling that the poems offered a "perennial source of happiness." They

> seemed to draw from a source of inward joy, of sympathetic
> and imaginative pleasure, which could be shared in by all
> human beings; which had no connexion with struggle or
> imperfection, but would be made richer by every improvement
> in the physical or social condition of mankind.... [T]here was
> real, permanent happiness in tranquil contemplation. (Mill,
> 91)

By Mill's account, then, Wordsworth found not only the eternal in Nature,
but the source of human vitality in the relationship with Nature. By
implication, the diminution of strength in the current that connects the
person and Nature diminishes whatever it is that makes for excitement.

When critics talk about Wordsworth's "bad" poetry, about his
"decline" or "desiccation," they are complaining less about his
reactionary views and more that the verse is dusty and dull, lacking
imagination and vibrancy. Ironically the subject of a great deal of this
poetry is the problem of living without excitement. Much of *The
Excursion*, for example, concerns how it is to live as a mechanism
alienated from the passionate bond with Nature rather than an organism
rooted in Nature, able to rely on grounding in Nature for vital fertility.
For Wordsworth, living without excitement is living without an organic
connection to Nature. Being estranged from Nature means being
estranged from the vital energy of excitement. Perhaps what accounts
for the failure of Wordsworth's later poetry is just such an estrangement
from nature. He sees it as a general malaise. In his well-known sonnet,
"The World Is Too Much With Us," Wordsworth expresses the new
dilemma of the early nineteenth century: Mankind freed from the
tyranny and deprivations of the *ancient regime*, nevertheless is not closer
to humanity:

> Getting and spending we lay waste our powers
> Little we see in nature that is ours.
> We have given our hearts away, a sordid boon!
> The sea that bares her bosom to the moon;
> The winds that will be howling at all hours,
> Are all up-gathered now like sleeping flowers;
> For this, for everything we are out of tune;
> It moves us not.

For himself, after the turn of the century, Wordsworth might have inverted the faith of his youth when he

> Was inwardly prepared to turn aside
> From law and custom and entrust himself
> To Nature for the happy end of all,
>   The Prelude, IX. 602–604

and fittingly say that he "was inwardly prepared to turn aside from Nature and entrust himself to law and custom for the happy end of all."

v.

The turn of the century was a turning point for Wordsworth, too.
After the publication of *Lyrical Ballads* in 1798, Wordsworth and Dorothy traveled to Germany with Coleridge. Leaving him to his own ways the brother and sister took poor lodgings in Goslar and stayed through the winter. It was a period of immense productivity for Wordsworth, a period when his youth came to full maturity and a fledgling maturity revealed itself.

Among the flood of poetry Wordsworth produced in the late 1790s and the first two years of the nineteenth century preceding his marriage are a series of love lyrics written in Goslar in which the beloved is called "Lucy." Many serious readers of Wordsworth's poetry consider these lyrics to be expressions of Wordsworth's impassioned love for Dorothy. (Reiman, 142, 643) Their argument has weight. In "The Glow-worm," dated April 12, 1802, shortly before his marriage to Mary Hutchinson, Wordsworth wrote

> Among all lovely things my Love had been;
> Had noted well the stars, all flowers that grew
> About her home; but she had never seen
> A Glow-worm, never one, and this I knew
>
> ....
> I led my Lucy to the spot, "Look Here!"
> Oh! Joy it was for her, and joy for me!

Dorothy copied out this poem and sent it to Mary Hutchinson in a letter dated April 16. Mary's sister, Sara transcribed the poem and substituted

"Mary" for "Lucy," a reasonable assumption, considering the impending marriage, but apparently a wrong one. Also on April 16, Wordsworth himself sent a copy of the poem to Coleridge and noted, "The incident of this Poem took place about seven years ago between Dorothy and me" (Johnston, 636). Using this evidence, and a statement by Coleridge that "A Slumber Did My Spirit Seal," in Ernest de Selincourt's words, "was written to suggest what W[ordsworth] would have felt on the death of his sister," it is fair to conclude that the Lucy of the Lucy poems is a figure standing in for Dorothy onto whom Wordsworth could project or displace the passionate love he felt for his sister. (Reiman, 156) The poems express not only love but also anxiety, describing the tension between approach and prevention. In "Strange Fits of Passion Have I Known," Wordsworth writes:

> When she I loved looked every day
> Fresh as a rose in June
> I to her cottage bent my way,
> Beneath an evening moon.

He continues in the next four stanzas to describe his mounting excitement as he approaches Lucy's cottage, an excitement mixed with a rising dread:

> With quickening pace my horse drew nigh
> Those paths so dear to me.
>
>   And now we reached the orchard-plot
> And, as we climbed the hill,
> The sinking moon to Lucy's cot
> Came near, and nearer still.

And then there is a sudden drop:

> My horse moved on; hoof after hoof
> He raised and never stopped:
> When down behind the cottage roof.
> At once, the bright moon dropped.

What fond and wayward thoughts will slide
Into a lover's head!
"O mercy!" to myself I cried,
"If Lucy should be dead!"

Each of the four following "Lucy poems" ends with a similar encounter with death rather than with the beloved, confirming the truth of the premonition which ends the first poem. Further adding to the sense that there were incestuous demons defining the relationship between William and Dorothy are a number of other of Wordsworth's poems, especially "Nutting," Dorothy's letters from the winter of 1798–1799 when the two lived in Goslar, and Dorothy's debilitating agitation in 1802 on William and Mary's wedding day:

> [T]he night before the wedding ... Dorothy ... put the wedding ring [William would give Mary] on her forefinger when she went to bed. Next morning she dressed herself all in bridal white and returned the ring to William for the ceremony. But he first slipped it back on her third finger and "blessed [her] fervently." Dorothy succumbed to a fit of hysteria and threw herself down as if dead until the small party returned from the church at eight o'clock in the morning. She went out to meet them as they returned, but again was overcome and had to be led back to the house. (Johnston, 788)

In addition to the poetic sublimations he accomplished in the Lucy poems, Wordsworth "drafted the beginning of an essay on morals" which lays out a defense for the direction his poetry and his thought would take for the rest of his life. In this essay, according to Johnston,

> Wordsworth argues that poetry and art can do more to change men's moral behavior than "such books as Mr. Godwyn's, Mr. Paley's & those of that whole tribe of authors" [advocating social reform]. These authors, unlike poets, "contain no picture of human life; they *describe* nothing." Their "bald & naked reasoning [are] impotent over our habits" unlike "a tale of distress," which can

"incorporate itself with the blood & vital juices of our minds." ... [Wordsworth] declares poetry more socially effective than philosophy. Men will never be *reasoned* into good actions ... but they may be *moved* to them by powerful images. If we understood this process better, Wordsworth concludes, we might be enabled "to be practically useful by informing [ourselves] how men placed in such situations will necessarily act, & thence enabling us to apply ourselves to the means of turning them into a more beneficial course, if necessary, or of giving them new ardour & knowledge when they are proceeding as they ought." (Johnston 636)

There was one other consideration that had a determining effect on Wordsworth's poetry: his need for money and, therefore, a need for his work to be acceptable in the market place. When the poet Robert Southey reviewed *Lyrical Ballads* unfavorably, Wordsworh wrote to Cottle, his publisher—after exclaiming, "I am in want of money."— complaining about the bad review. Southey, he argues,

knew that money was of importance to me. If he could not conscientiously have spoken differently of the volume, he ought to have declined the task of reviewing it... I care little for the praise of any other professional critic, but as it may help me to pudding. (Johnston, 674–5)

Other reviews were not as harsh. "Tintern Abbey" was generally praised. Over other poems critics were divided. "The Mad Mother" became a popular hit and was even incorporated into a melodrama called *Pizarro* when it opened at the Drury Lane, recited by Dorothy Jordan, a leading actress of the day. (Johnston, 675) But critics did not favor "The Rhyme of the Ancient Mariner," one of Coleridge's contributions to the anonymous volume. Charles Burney—the father of John Keats's beloved, Fanny—objected to the gloominess of *Lyrical Ballads* and to its "implied criticism of the social system," specifically citing several poems, which Wordsworth altered accordingly. (Johnston, 676) Even more significantly, Wordsworth moved "The Ancient Mariner" which had been the first poem in the 1798 edition, to the back of the book in 1800, replacing it with the merrier "Expostulation and Reply" and "The Tables Turned." He needed income from the book.

VI.

Simple as some of his lyrics and naïve as some of his ballads may seem, neither Wordsworth the man nor the body of his poetry is simple. Wordsworth reconfigured pieces of his life through his poetry, including several forbidden loves. He promoted social, spiritual, political and metaphysical agendas. He rewrote much of his verse throughout his life so that his poems are not time-bound but take on the textures of shifting consciousness, especially since many can be read in their several versions. The reciprocal relation of perceiver and perceived also defines the nature of the relation between the poetry and the reader. Like "Proteus rising from the sea" Wordsworth's poetry cannot be forced into one shape or pinned down. Our consciousness must wrestle with it. He varied his style from verse that sings nearly like a nursery rhyme in "Peter Bell" or "Simon Lee," or "We Are Seven" to rolling chords of Miltonic blank verse and winding syntax in *The Prelude*. His supreme mastery of the sonnet form is evident by the grace with which he moved through the constraining structure without a strain, steadily, surely and precisely, sometimes beautifully, saying exactly what he means to. He was a wild child of nature, both introspective as a youth and a firebrand. He aged into a conservative country gentleman with a government sinecure who left off limning the lives of common people and the morally uplifting radical pathos of their existence for phenomenological examinations of his own mind, memory, perception and consciousness. His poetry ascended from being rooted in the poet's perception of Nature to a transcendental contemplation and abstraction. Compare these two sonnets, the first, "Composed upon Westminster Bridge, September 3, 1802," from the golden decade of his greatness; the second, from the fourteen sonnet sequence defending capital punishment, *Upon the Punishment of Death*, from only nine years before his own death in 1850 at the age of eighty.

> Earth has not anything to show more fair:
> Dull would he be of soul who could pass by
> A sight so touching in its majesty:
> This City now doth, like a garment, wear
> The beauty of the morning; silent, bare,
> Ships, towers, domes, theatres, and temples lie

Open unto the fields, and to the sky;
All bright and glittering in the smokeless air.
Never did sun more beautifully steep
In his first splendour, valley, rock, or hill;
Ne'er saw I, never felt, a calm so deep!
The river glideth at his own sweet will:
Dear God! the very houses seem asleep;
And all that mighty heart is lying still!

* * *

Is 'Death,' when evil against good has fought
With such fell mastery that a man may dare
By deeds the blackest purpose to lay bare?
Is Death, for one to that condition brought,
For him, or any one, the thing that ought
To be 'most' dreaded? Lawgivers, beware,
Lest, capital pains remitting till ye spare
The murderer, ye, by sanction to that thought
Seemingly given, debase the general mind;
Tempt the vague will tried standards to disown,
Nor only palpable restraints unbind,
Whose absolute rule permits not to withstand
In the weak love of life his least command.

The abstraction at the end of the first sonnet is a metaphor arising from the concrete imagery of the poem. Wordsworth shows the body of the city. From that, he derives its heart. Syntactically, the sonnet unfolds in a sequence of direct declaratives, entirely end-stopped in the first two lines and with the meaning only lightly sliding over the line when there is enjambment in the following lines. His eye is steadily on the object, and consequently, so is the reader's. The emotion that moves us moves us to co-experience with the poet. The sonnet form is the engine driving the poetry. It is its music.

The fourth poem of the *Punishment* sequence begins with two abstractions, and the poem is never grounded in concrete things, rather it speaks of "evil," "good," "fell mastery," "purpose," "condition," "the thing that ought to be," "sanction to that thought," "general mind," "Honor." Rather than being direct and declarative, the syntax is serpentine and qualified. The opening sestet until the transition at the end of the sixth line is composed of two interrogatives, the second repeating the first in order to finish what its argumentative and oratorical rhetoric prevented from being cased in one sentence. The thundering repetition of the "is" compels us to listen, and the quantity of qualifiers—"when," "with," "that," "by," "for"—asks us to follow an argument whose syntax represents it as airtight. The octet, beginning "Lawyers, beware," commences as a warning and becomes a sermon listing unwanted ends should the sonnet's message go unheeded. The machinery of the sonnet tends to validate its argument. A rhetorical question is posed. The consequences of not heeding the speaker are exposed. The argument is clinched by the resolution contained in a rhymed couplet. One can greatly admire the skill of the sonnet and the command of rhetoric and linguistic dexterity it possesses, and if one is a partisan of Wordsworth's position, one's forces may feel rallied, but the touch of the other sonnet is not there. Even this, however, to Wordsworth's credit, is not the accident of failing power, but seems the willful decision of an intellect that came to see constraint more necessary than liberty. Wordsworth moved with the times. In the 1790's revolt against constraint appeared to him to serve human dignity and liberty. Recoiling from its excesses, and retreating from the dangerous turbulence of his own passion should it be admitted, in his last decades, containment, custom and ceremony appeared to him to be the props essential for the exercise of liberty. He had seen the dissolution that indulgence had provoked in Coleridge, defeated by desire and opium; he had endured the death of two of his children and the furious illness of his sister. His eye had moved from nature to the supernatural. In the tenth *Punishment* sonnet he admonishes not to measure "Infinite Power, perfect Intelligence," by "finite sense."

Wordsworth was a master of the two qualities Matthew Arnold cites Goethe as calling necessary for poetry, "the indispensable mechanical part," and the part that "shows spirituality and feeling ... soul and matter." Sometimes he achieved both in the same verses. Those are his masterworks. Sometimes he achieved only one or the other. In his later verse, even if the spirit failed, Wordsworth adhered to the "boundaries and wholesome regulative laws, under which excellent work may ... be produced." Taken as a poet of anthology pieces, Wordsworth can be flawless. Taken as the architect of a vast body of work of disparate quality, he shows the greatness of a poet, searching through Nature and in Thought, whose work describes the character and contours of several eras and the interrelation of opposing times. Much like Marcel Proust in his recollection of lost time, Wordsworth presents the phenomenology of a mind alive in nature, culture and his times, responding to them and to itself.

NOTES

1. All quotations from *The Prelude* are taken from the text of 1805, edited by Ernest de Selincourt, revised impression by Helen Darbishire, in *Wordsworth: The Prelude, or Growth of A Poet's Mind* (London: Oxford University Press, 1960).

2. Of his prose, too. Writing in 1835, and entrenched in his conservatism, Wordsworth was arguing for what would today be called "welfare rights" for poor people. See "Postscript" in *CPW: Wordsworth*, X, 117–118.

3. In the ninety-eighth stanza of the third canto of *Don Juan*, Byron reverses the general acceptance of some dull passages in even great works:
We learn from Horace, 'Homer sometimes sleeps';
We feel without him,—Wordsworth sometimes wakes.

WORKS CITED

Arnold, Matthew. *The Portable Matthew Arnold*, ed. Lionel Trilling. New York: The Viking Press, 1949.

Bradley, A. C. "Wordsworth," *Oxford Lectures on Poetry*. London: Macmillan and Co., Ltd., 1941.

Darbishire, Helen. *Wordsworth: The Prelude, or Growth of A Poet's Mind*. London: Oxford University Press, 1960.

Erdman, David V. "Wordsworth as Heartsworth; or, was Regicide the Prophetic Ground of Those 'Moral Questions'?" in *The Evidence of the Imagination: Studies of Interactions Between Life and Art in English Romantic Literature*, ed. Donald H. Reiman et al. (New York: New York University Press, 1978).

Gill, Stephen. *William Wordsworth: A Life*. Oxford: Clarendon Press, 1989.

Hartman, Geoffrey H. *Wordsworth's Poetry, 1787–1814*. New Haven: Yale University Press, 1971.

Johnston, Kenneth R. *The Hidden Wordsworth: Poet, Lover, Spy*. New York: W.W. Norton & Company, 1998.

McFarland, Thomas. "Wordsworth's Dessication," in *William Wordsworth: Intensity and Achievement*. Oxford: Clarendon Press, 1992.

Mills, John Stuart. *Essential Works of John Stuart Mill*, ed. Max Lerner. New York: Bantam Books, 1965.

Reiman, Donald H. "Poetry of Familiarity: Wordsworth, Dorothy, and Mary Hutchinson" in *The Evidence of the Imagination: Studies of Interactions between Life and Art in English Romantic Literature*, ed. Donald H. Reiman et al. (New York: New York University Press, 1978).

Wordsworth, William. *The Complete Poetical Works of William Wordsworth*. Boston: Houghton Mifflin Company, 1911.

GEOFFREY H. HARTMAN

The Excursion

THE ONE GREAT DEFECT

Concerning *The Excursion*, the worst has already been said by Jeffrey, Hazlitt, and others. One must admit that to read carefully its nine books is a massively depressing experience, and it is hard to think of a corrective for *that* despondency. Though a radical slenderizing would save *The Excursion* from dying (like a dinosaur) of its own weight, nothing can remove the haunting suspicion that it is a second-rate work which might have continued *Paradise Regained* to become the greatest humanistic poem in the language. The betrayal of possible sublimity is impossible to forgive; for even if we exclude Book I and passages originating in Wordsworth's prime, there are still in the remainder of the poem tokens of a habitual poetic greatness that preserve it from settling to the splendor of a period piece. Yet, however condescending and ungrateful it is to diagnose failure, an understanding of where Wordsworth fails (rather than, immediately, why) may disencumber his poem of that mass of conjecture which failure as well as success brings on.

The Excursion offers us not a vision, but a voice. Its failure, and to some extent its distinction, reside in that. In Milton also, as Macaulay noted, the imaginative impact is mediated by aural rather than by visual suggestions. From Milton we receive, to put it plainly, the vision of a

From *Wordsworth's Poetry* (Yale University Press, 1964). © 1964 by Geoffrey Hartman. Reprinted by permission of the author.

voice—its power, the power of the Word reverberating for good or bad. But Milton still orients us graphically by using a very simple kind of myth and cosmos. It is simple, at least, when compared to Dante's. There are subtlety and precision in Milton, but on a massive scale; and the reader need only accept a few imaginative axes. Hell, for instance, is not the opposite of heaven but its parody; so that Satan's pain is the remembrance of light forever lost, and the mocking presence of "No light, but rather darkness visible." It follows easily enough that the hope buoying Satan is a false hope, and, like the light, a real Tantalus punishment. In this way Milton elaborates his imaginary world by means of a few graphic axioms.

Now *The Excursion*, however low we rank it, has an aim not unlike these greater poems; yet its visionary element is almost denuded of visual supports. After the first book (this reservation will come often) the visual and visionary divide, the first being curiously neglected, and the second being rendered by an oblique and self-conscious voice. The Wanderer only occasionally makes us feel the earth he stands on or the heaven he stands under, and for whose sake he sermonizes:

> —Voiceless the stream descends into the gulf
> With timid lapse;—and lo! while in this strait
> I stand—the chasm of sky above my head
> Is heaven's profoundest azure; no domain
> For fickle, short-lived clouds to occupy,
> Or to pass through; but rather an abyss
> In which the everlasting stars abide. (III.92–98)

Such moments are a welcome relief to the effusions of this strange old man, who instead of letting silence speak, as it does powerfully through Leech-gatherer or Cumberland Beggar, betrays it. The visionary element of the poem should fuse with "the speaking face of Nature," yet after Book I it is increasingly an abstract voice that carries the burden of vision, and, as it were, stoops to the visual or to nature. Sometimes, in fact, Nature ironically punctuates the Wanderer's speech with its truly visionary sounds:

> List!—I heard,
> From yon huge breast of rock, a voice sent forth
> As if the visible mountain made the cry.
> Again! (IV.402–05)

Wordsworth's separation of visionary and visual results usually in the atrophy of both. It is a further step in his flight from the autonomous imagination. His flight could also, of course, have led *into* the visual. Those who "peep and botanize" on their mother's grave, or whose dull eye hangs on its object in brute slavery (IV.1254), are refugees from their own mind. But Wordsworth, unlike these, never denies the power of imagination. On the contrary, imagination has something sacred about it, which is why he hesitates to come near. Though *The Excursion* is predicated on the possibility of natural visionary experience ("his spirit shaped / Her prospects, nor did he believe,—he *saw*"), and though such experience is given as proof of the argument that man's imagination can bind itself fruitfully to the world, Wordsworth shies from entering the area of his greatness. By removing himself as much as possible from the immediacy of his senses, and especially of the eye, he omits the sphere where imagination may seize on the seen and make it a haunting image, a "questionable shape." He reverts to lecturing on a venerable discipline, that of the Platonic-Christian journey from visible to invisible, from the *res factae* (Romans 1:19–20) to the intuition of an active principle "howe'er removed /From sense and observation ... " (IX.3–4)

Yet poetry is distinguished from even the most poetical philosophy by the fact that it exists only where a poet is led beyond his thoughts. He *enters* his poem, like Dante or Milton. Dante is "guided," and Milton "flies" on wings for which he asks support in the words of the Prophet: "Instruct me, for Thou know'st." If Wordsworth flies, it is from open vision, like Jonah or his own Solitary. What he and his sufferers see we never entirely learn; their vision is subsumed, veiled like a holy thing which might break out. The power of vision, and its fearful or pacifying effects on the human person, are rendered by him; but rarely the substance. Vision, in this poem, is always a suffering, whether conceived in joy or in pain: for the soul is raised by it to a height it cannot keep, and the human energies striving to regain that height fall into despondency and thence into an "appetite of death." (It is sometimes asked what Lear dies of, whether from thinking his daughter is alive, or from the realization that she is dead. But surely he dies, like Gloucester, of imagination. Lear, imagining Cordelia is alive, cannot bear to fall from that height. So it is with Wordsworth's sufferers.)

The poet's Right from vision causes a warp of obliquity felt throughout *The Excursion*. It lends him strength for the story of

Margaret, which he unfolds with preternatural slowness, yet wearies us elsewhere, because we are always brought close to some substantial drama, yet never allowed to see it. Milton again proceeds very differently. While saying "Dream not of other Worlds" (*Paradise Lost*, VIII.175), he nevertheless dreams of them, purging our unearthliness by indulging it, or substituting a clearer vision for a murky. Wordsworth, however, fails to respect his earlier conviction that

> Dumb yearnings, hidden appetites, are ours,
> And they *must* have their food. (*Prelude* V.506–07)

Though we infer the existence of such yearnings from the tragic stories included in *The Excursion*, inference by itself is no satisfaction for the soul, which needs at least an admixture of direct vision, that "taste of eternity" hope adds to faith. The defect of *The Excursion* (after the first book especially) is to *show* us death and to *word* hope. Only the story of Margaret, the purest example of Wordsworth's art, uses inference successfully; it reveals the indomitableness of a woman's hope by showing the death of whatever she abandons in that hope.

Wordsworth's flight from vision may be a simple orthodox trembling or the result of a terror like that of the Prophets. *The Excursion* is less free of religious scruple than *The Prelude*, and often comes close to supporting Dr. Johnson's caveat about religious poetry. Yet understanding Wordsworth's fear, we can lay the ghost of the charge that he averts his face from "half of human ken." It is not from man that Wordsworth turns but from the apocalyptic response to his mortality. Margaret and the Wanderer share a too vivid sense of mortal being. The Wanderer, nevertheless, keeps his imagination actively linked to the earth, but Margaret falls prey to *secret love*, to a near-apocalyptic displacement of hope.

The verse prospectus to *The Excursion*, therefore, though an epic flyting, is no bravado. The poet passes unalarmed the myths of traditional apocalyptic poetry because the mind in its daily working creates things more awful than these. Previous imaginings of terror or beauty merely adumbrated what the mind achieves naturally when wedded in love to this world, or what it imagines and suffers when divorced from it. The story of Margaret certainly breeds such fear and awe "As fall upon us often when we look / Into our Minds, into the Mind

of Man." The poem declines, however, into a massive communion with
the dead, noble raptures spoken above their graves. It is the living mind
and the live moment we need communion with, not the storied dust of
the dead.

While the figure of the Solitary still redeems Books II and III, the
next book initiates a funeral sermon on human aspirations, and VI and
VII ("The Churchyard among the Mountains") add an involuntary
parody of the epic *nekya* or descent to the dead. I doubt that there exists
another poem of such length in which death and tragic mutation
become so literally the ground of the whole. The intended locus, of
course, is the mind of man; which contemplates and is not cast down,
which recognizes in suffering the disabled passion of hope. Death
cannot be winged, however, and it is a realized impotence—"I blessed
her in the impotence of grief" (I.924)—that is truer here to strength of
heart than the joint fluencies of Pastor and Wanderer.

GENRE, SUBJECT, AND ARGUMENT

The Excursion is a strongly consistent poem in terms of genre, subject,
and argument. All three are deeply meditated, and the genre in
particular is a difficult blending of new and old that needs clarification.
It certainly has roots in the topographical and contemplative poetry of
the eighteenth century. Thomson, Akenside, Cowper, and Dyer are
ancestors of note. Their poetry, in turn, is best seen as a development of
the *Georgics*, a poem containing the same attention to country lore, a
similarly loose yet didactic structure, and a respect for the mind that
remains close to "the great and permanent objects that act upon it." But
the ambulatory scheme, as well as the compression of time (though into
five days rather than a single day) owe something to Milton's *Il Penseroso*
and *L'Allegro*, which influenced Wordsworth as early as "The Vale of
Esthwaite." Wordsworth seems to return to a first line of development
starting with his earliest long-poem venture, affecting *Descriptive
Sketches* and *An Evening Walk*, and interrupted, as it were, by his
experiment in autobiography.

Why did the *Georgics* and associated poems appeal to
Wordsworth? That they dealt with man's relation to nature is less
important than that Virgilian nature is a *divinity* which has to be wooed
and wounded, conquered and worshiped, at the same time. The sense of

Nature as a living and unpredictable presence, now gracious now fearful, emerges already from Thomson's *Seasons*, which are strongly imitative of Virgil. Yet Thomson, like Dryden in his translation of the *Georgics*, too often substitutes poetic machinery for divine. Though he is especially good in the ominous parts, we admire him more for the energy or luster of his language than for the actual subject. The style of a didactic poem, said Joseph Warton, "ought certainly to abound in the most bold and forcible metaphors, the most glowing and picturesque epithets, it ought to be elevated and enlivened ... by every figure that can lift a language above the vulgar and current expressions."

Virgil's brilliance, needless to say, is also not subdued to his subject, but he has an inestimable advantage over his seventeenth- and eighteenth-century imitators. The body of knowledge he deals with has not yet "selved" from myth; cult and cultivation are still close to each other. For Dryden and Thomson, however, agriculture as such is a recalcitrant theme and practically divorced from folklore or myth: it is a subject that can only reveal the energy of the contemplating mind. Thomson, in fact, in a poem much freer of its original than a translation could ever be, clearly shifts the ground of interest from cultivation to culture of mind. The cult of nature is pursued only insofar as it raises the mind above nature.

Wordsworth's "labor" is also primarily an attention to nature that yields imaginative fruits. The *agricola* now is the poet himself, who observes how nature has fructified imagination. And, like the true farmer, he observes or analyzes not for the sake of analysis but in order to take advantage of the earth. His past life, which he so carefully husbands in *The Prelude*, is analogous to the body of myth or knowledge garnered by Virgil, and presented by him as a token of hope. Despite the divinity of nature, its unpredictable and even "monstrous" behavior, labor is repaid, the earth is grateful. If the future is like the past, adds Wordsworth, nature will fructify imagination now as then. Thomson does not reach this simple and highest theme. He labors nature to extract from it natural religion, and though Wordsworth is by no means free of the habit, it remains subordinate. Whether or not nature leads the mind to God, it suffices imagination. This seems to him the greater miracle.

The conception developed from the *Georgics*, that nature is the proper ground of man's imagination as well as of his labor, was only as influential as the form of the poem. Virgil's manual is devoid of action in the ordinary sense. So is *The Excursion*. Virgil can build his poem on the four branches of husbandry, and within each book follows the seasons or weaves together admonition and myth. Wordsworth, of course, structures his narrative less didactically and adopts once again the frame of a country walk. This frame, however, allows him to link story to story in the Virgilian manner, i.e. like a poet who is still essentially a combiner of legends. Wordsworth, like Burns, attaches his imagination to folklore, and in this he continues the tradition of Chaucer, Spenser, and Shakespeare more securely than the purely myth-making poet.

Yet he succeeds only partially, after *Lyrical Ballads*, in staying in touch with folklore and "local superstition." He is perhaps too interested in the workings of the naive mind and not enough in the person whose mind it is. Wordsworth's natural metaphors are important enough to found a whole theory of imagination, yet too thin to satisfy imagination itself. The Idiot Boy's "and the sun did shine so cold" or the poor woman's "that waggon does not care for us" are telling cries, with something of the economy and density of the repressed imagination, yet the pressure of Shakespeare's mind engenders them continually. Chaucer and Shakespeare are often greater poets of natural life than Wordsworth; they know nature is a constipated or frozen form of imagination and refuse to worship its randomness. The poet, said Shakespeare, is "of imagination all compact"; but lack of compactness so distinguished Wordsworth from other great poets that John Stuart Mill called him the poet of unpoetical natures.

It is nevertheless true that the stories, reflections, and conversations of *The Excursion* are strongly linked to *place*, and are in that sense natural. Wordsworth raises them from an inert landscape as a magician does rabbits. The living memory sees something merged with nature, a disused well, a discarded book, a grave. In this unapparent or quiet vestige, Wanderer and Pastor recognize a story that is all too human. Nature is potentially humanized; there is nothing which does not declare *man* to the excursive and meditative mind. "All things shall speak of Man," says Wordsworth in an early passage, revised for *The Excursion*. And going back still further, to the lispings of "The Vale of Esthwaite," we find the alienated poet ("doubting what to call his own") wandering in fancy around the vale of his lost childhood, seeking to read nature, and to draw a tale from every rock. In *The Excursion* also, it is not an ideal but a storied landscape he discovers.

Yet, as the poem proceeds, and more ghosts are raised, nature takes on the aspect of a large graveyard. Only the creative memory, or the excursive mind, can see it as anything else. The emphasis is shifted, by the momentum of the poem, from the individual fates that are charactered, to the more comprehensive question of how a man can face death or mutability and remain uninjured. Wanderer and Pastor appear then as examples of the uninjured mind (IX.784). Their strength lies not in the ejaculative piety the age demands but in the way they confront and subsume death. It is their mind, or rather the quality of their imagination, that matters, and the stories they revive are never told for their own sakes. There is no riot in them, no "vain dalliance with the misery / Even of the dead" (I.628); nothing is told merely to pleasure the time. The stories of Wanderer and Pastor are drawn from nature (specific place) and return to it; they are products of imagination blended with spirit of place, and endow nature paradigmatically with some of the richness of interest necessary to keep imagination well-grounded.

Wordsworth's subject, then, is the mind of man—the uninjured mind. At the dramatic center of the poem stands the Solitary: can his mind be restored to health? Wordsworth is honest enough not to resolve the question. We do not know, by the end of the poem, what breach has been made in the Solitary's despair. The Solitary almost steals the show, opposing his own *mens immota*, his sense of injured merit, to the contrary firmness of Wanderer and Pastor. His instinctive movements toward retreat (V.73, VIII.30) are, after all, not so different from the Wanderer's tendency toward repose. When the latter talks of "the sublime attractions of the grave" it is hard to tell the unction of the phrase from its imaginative daring. Each of these friendly opponents has a fixed faith which is not always distinguishable from the fixity of death.

In pitting Solitary against Wanderer, Pastor, and Poet, somewhat like Job against his three friends, Wordsworth came very close to creating a poem of true spiritual debate. That he did not succeed better is due to a variety of causes; but the lineaments of the conception are there, and often mock the finished product. The Solitary is to be delivered from Despair, and *The Excursion* is therefore linked thematically with Book I, canto ix, of the *Faerie Queene*, Book X of *Paradise Lost*, and Wordsworth's own crisis described in *Prelude* X ff. As in Spenser, Despair causes a wish to escape the human condition. Self-annihilation seems preferable to self-confrontation, and it could be achieved by a return to mere nature ("sleep / Doth, in my estimate of good, appear / A better state than waking; death than sleep: / Feelingly sweet is stillness after storm") or by the abandonment of reality for pure vision. The Red Cross Knight, taken up the holy mountain and shown the New Jerusalem, does not want to descend, and has to be reminded of his mission and georgic origin. The Solitary has a similar mountain experience.

But, unlike Spenser or Milton, Wordsworth wishes to combat despair by purely human arguments. It is almost as if he meant to humanize his predecessors. The Wanderer, clearly, is a champion of natural wisdom; and though his arguments are supplemented by the Pastor's, and these are doctrinally phrased, both afford the Solitary the same kind of comfort. Starting at opposite points, from experience and from revelation, Wanderer and Pastor arrive at one conclusion, and blend their voices in thanksgiving. It is unfortunate, however, that the poet, to realize this plan, must give the Wanderer (who supposedly takes his wisdom from "mute insensate things,") the eloquence of a preacher. Equally unfortunate is the fact that religion and eloquence are still close enough so that as the Wanderer waxes in eloquence he also grows in religion. The poem, instead of keeping to the dilemma of the Solitary, becomes on occasion a defense of the Established Church.

Despite this betrayal of subject, *The Excursion* continues *Paradise Regained* in the same way as the *Prelude* dovetails *Paradise Lost*. It is "Recover'd Paradise" that Wordsworth, anticipating the blissful hour, means to sing. He ranges through the "highth or depth of nature's bounds." The deeds he sings of can be qualified as "Above Heroic, though in secret done." The increasing Miltonisms, moreover, seem to me to derive more from Milton's later style, which attempts no more than a "middle flight." But more important, perhaps, than the connection with *Paradise Regained* is the deeply fortuitous link with Dante's *Purgatorio*. It is not my purpose to salvage Wordsworth's poem by giving it a sublime context. Yet having considered its genre and subject, we come, finally to the "argument," and this does run parallel to Dante's. Not only is Earthly Paradise the crown of this part of Dante's journey as of Wordsworth's, but the sins purged are essentially those of *disordered love*. "Set love in order, thou that lovest me," is the verse of Francis of Assisi on which, according to E. G. Gardner, *Purgatorio* rests. In Wordsworth it would be more exact to talk of disordered hope or

imagination; it is the unredeemed strength of hope and the ravage of too
intense imagination for which Margaret, the Solitary, and the Solitary's
wife suffer:

> the innocent Sufferer often sees
> Too clearly; feels too vividly; and longs
> To realize the vision, with intense
> And over-constant yearning;—there—there lies
> The excess, by which the balance is destroyed.
> (IV.174–78)

Imagination itself is the illness. It is also, of course, the strength of
man. Margaret's hope in her husband's return is so fierce that it
withdraws her from all life. Like an unweaned child she is "unwilling to
be fed" by aught else. If the poet, at the end of the Wanderer's tale, is so
moved that he cannot thank the old man, but turns aside and blesses
Margaret with "a brother's love," it is less because the touch of suffering
makes him kin than because he has recognized, through her, the
visionary power of hope: a power in which he shares for good or evil.

Despair being related to the vigor of imagination, Wordsworth can
give no facile antidotes. He begins, in fact, with the example of a
despondency that was not able to be "corrected." Margaret dies desolate.
The Solitary remains, at the end of the poem, a moot case. The Pastor's
examples of the calming or strengthening influences of nature are also
not without their complexities. Wordsworth knows he is dealing with a
"sickness unto death" coterminous with the best and strongest part of
man. "Oh, Sir! the good die first, / And they whose hearts are dry as
summer dust / Burn to the socket" (I.500–02). No wonder Shelley
remembered these lines and made them part of the preface to *Alastor*.
The poet's reaction to the Wanderer's story shows that the consolation
must come from the same source as the grief, from a recognition of the
supernatural vigor of desire, hope, imagination.

What, then, except blind faith leads Wordsworth to think the
imagination can ever be naturalized? If hope, says the poet in his verse
preface, truly blends with the world, despondency or visionary despair
will cease, the earth will satisfy imagination wholly, and be as Paradise
Regained. Yet Margaret shows rather the inhuman or too human
strength of hope. Here we touch on something in the poem that has not

been fully understood. It is not Margaret or the other sufferers who prove that Wordsworth's faith is not misplaced. It is the Wanderer: the quality of his mind, the way he faces human suffering, and the genealogy of his strength. Wordsworth's anticipatory poem, his "spousal verse," rests on this simple man, bred simply, a pedlar by profession, and not exceptional in any point of provenance or fate.

BOOK I: THE WANDERER

The Wanderer's attention is exquisitely directed toward nature. He has the same eye for detail as the Sea Captain of "The Thorn," and perhaps the same imagination of disaster, but his pacing of the tale is perfect, and shows a restraint which speaks the habitual quality of a mind familiar with evidences of death and neither shunning nor anticipating them. His "realism" thus assumes an energy and morality of its own. He looks at nature as a seer, and what he sees is linked startlingly with death—"I see around me here / Things which you cannot see: we die, my Friend, / Nor we alone ..." (I.469–71). This leap of the imagination is among the finest things in the book, not only because (as in Shakespeare) it betrays the prophetic soul, but because the Wanderer rarely allows himself such inner haste. Though the passion of Margaret is deeply moving, we are equally affected by the Old Man's ability to keep his eye on death, and to describe, with an intensity of sight so purged that nothing morbid or sentimental remains, the gradual extinction of a human soul. His is the strength lacking in Margaret's husband, who cannot bear to look on the misery of his loved ones.

The poet shares in this "harvest of a quiet eye." The subdued visual intensity of the whole first book shows that Wordsworth is refusing to stand in the service of "that beauty, which, as Milton sings, / Hath terror in it" (*Prelude* XIV.245–46). The poem's opening landscape exemplifies his restraint:

> 'Twas summer, and the sun had mounted high:
> Southward the landscape indistinctly glared
> Through a pale steam; but all the northern downs,
> In clearest air ascending, showed far off
> A surface dappled o'er with shadows flung
> From brooding clouds; shadows that lay in spots

> Determined and unmoved, with steady beams
> Of bright and pleasant sunshine interposed;
> To him most pleasant who on soft cool moss
> Extends his careless limbs along the front
> Of some huge cave, whose rocky ceiling casts
> A twilight of its own, an ample shade,
> Where the wren warbles, while the dreaming man,
> Half conscious of the soothing melody,
> With side-long eye looks out upon the scene,
> By power of that impending covert thrown
> To finer distance. (I.1–17)

We move noticeably from high noon to the depth of a cavern, from which the eye returns to the scene, but soothed now by shade and melody and "finer distance." The texture of the passage is subtle, modulating starker intimations ("glared," "brooding," the half-felt personifications) or static properties (the shadows "determined and unmoved," the past tense and general dance of *d*'s) into a more purely picturesque, softened and reciprocally blended prospect. In the first version of this landscape from *An Evening Walk*,

> When, in the south, the wan noon, brooding still,
> Breath'd a pale steam around the glaring hill ...

not only is the personification more inclusive, but the rhyme, the fine jingle of "brooding" and "glaring," and the ritardando of "wan noon brooding" tense the very rhythm of the lines between stark-still and forward motion.

The visual theme is quickly attached to the person of the Wanderer. When we first see him his face is toward the setting sun, and the second time he lies supine, shaded from the noonday sun, his eyes half-shut. But there are also contrary indications, showing the unsubdued nature of his eye. "Time had compressed the freshness of his cheek / Into a narrower circle of deep red, / But had not tamed his eye" (I.426–28); "He had rehearsed / Her homely tale with such familiar power, / With such an active countenance, an eye / So busy ..." (I.614–17). His picture of Margaret speaks for itself:

evermore
Her eyelids drooped, her eyes downward were cast;
And, when she at her table gave me food,
She did not look at me. Her voice was low,
Her body was subdued. (I.791–95)

The Wanderer's spirit *clings* to Margaret, "so familiarly / Do I perceive her manner, and her look, / And presence" (I.780–82). But the essential difference between him and Margaret is that he has retained his excursive power; he is not bound up in vision but still pastures wide, letting nature wean his eyes. Nothing is more beautifully rendered than his broadening glance (I.710 ff.) that mounts gradually into recognition:

From the bench I rose;
But neither could divert nor soothe my thoughts.
The spot, though fair, was very desolate—
The longer I remained, more desolate:
And, looking round me, now I first observed
The comer stones, on either side the porch,
With dull red stains discoloured, and stuck o'er
With tufts and hairs of wool, as if the sheep,
That fed upon the Common, thither came
Familiarly, and found a couching-place
Even at her threshold. Deeper shadows fell
From these tall elms; the cottage-clock struck eight;—
I turned, and saw her distant a few steps. (I.738–50)

The Wanderer, clearly, possesses that chastity of recognition which Henry James' characters are in search of. To know, or even to desire to know, is connected with guilt. The visual theme passes here into a higher mode still based on the old cry for ocular proof. But the Wanderer restores to knowledge some of its innocence, its mixture of good, for even if knowledge is always of death, or of good and evil, his mind remains inviolate, and does not lust for what it knows it will find.

Wordsworth's lengthy account of the Wanderer's childhood (I.108 ff.) traces the genealogy of an inherently moral imagination. Brought up in nature, by nature, the Wanderer stands before us as the embodiment of natural wisdom. Although God-fearing parents and the Scottish

Church tended him closely, his religion sometimes seemed, the poet says, "Self-taught, as of a dreamer in the woods." He would be a mute inglorious poet had Wordsworth not come to make him speak too much. His mind is satisfied by nature, not now, in the moment, which may be evil or lacking, but because nature, instead of being an object or something alien "out there," is indistinguishable from his yet living past.

The Wanderer has known communions with nature too strong to be forgotten, moments of terror too stark to be entirely remembered, and silences too deep to be profaned. By weaning his senses and, in particular, his eyes, nature teaches him that he must separate from many things, yet offers him the compensation of an active spirit. As he grows, and is unsatisfied with dimmer perceptions than those that used to lie on his mind and perplex his bodily sense, he develops an ability to fasten images on his brain, and to raise, by meditation, their affective power. At the same time he turns eyes and ears outward, searching the external world, whose variety both rewards and draws him. Taking away one kind of food, and offering him another, nature gradually binds him to her in faith. He trusts her generosity and his power (through her) of renovation. He becomes what Wordsworth so aptly calls him, "A Being made / Of many Beings" (I.430–31).

The slow maturation of nature does not save the Wanderer from solitude or evil, but enables him to face these without exhaustion. "Disesteem of life" cannot reach him. Nature has made him so active toward her that he is endlessly renovated through an outward going. Like the Red Cross Knight after his trials and his passage through Caelia's House, the Wanderer is able to get up after each fall, to rebound. His ultimate reward is to look *through* death. "If the doors of perception were cleansed," says Blake, "everything would appear to man as it is; infinite." The Wanderer's home is with nature only insofar as it breathes "immortality, revolving life, / And greatness still revolving; infinite" (I.228–29). He is the proper antagonist for the Solitary, who lives sullen in the bosom of nature, and who makes his entry in Book II.

BOOKS II–III: THE SOLITARY

The Solitary has lost his "excursive power," and with it his chances to be renewed. After the death of his two children and his wife, the failure of his faith in political action, and the decay of earlier vitalities of feeling (all have correlatives in Wordsworth's life), he becomes a recluse, avoiding contact with other men and literally burying himself before his time. His place of abode is like an urn:

> We scaled, without a track to ease our steps,
> A steep ascent; and reached a dreary plain,
> With a tumultuous waste of huge hill tops
> Before us; savage region! which I paced
> Dispirited: when, all at once, behold!
> Beneath our feet, a little lowly vale,
> A lowly vale, and yet uplifted high
> Among the mountains; even as if the spot
> Had been from eldest time by wish of theirs
> So placed, to be shut out from all the world!
> Urn-like it was in shape, deep as an urn;
> With rocks encompassed, save that to the south
> Was one small opening, where a heath-clad ridge
> Supplied a boundary less abrupt and close;
> A quiet treeless nook, with two green fields,
> A liquid pool that glittered in the sun,
> And one bare dwelling; one abode, no more! (II.323–39)

This funereal place, almost naked of charms, attracts the poet strangely. The "dreary plain," a Miltonic phrase descriptive of Hell, now reveals "a sweet Recess" (II.349), which is what Adam calls Paradise on learning that he must leave it. As if to objectify some (not unattractive) thought of death, Poet and Wanderer hear voices rising in a dirge from that urn-shaped valley. By a significant prolepsis, voice precedes sight, and by a second prolepsis, the Wanderer, even before seeing the cortege, concludes that it is the Solitary who has died.

When, therefore, in the only dramatic surprise of the poem, the Solitary appears before them, it is a dead man they see. Practically his first words indicate the death-wish in him, "The hand of Death ... has been here; but could not well / Have fallen more lightly, if it had not fallen / Upon myself" (II.542–45). His confession in Book III then links the "appetite of death" with the desire for repose. The Solitary's remaining hope is that the current of his life will soon reach "The unfathomable gulf, where all is still!" (III.991).

Who is the Solitary, if not the Hamletian man in black, and a dangerous part of the poet's mind? In one of his earliest poems, "Lines left upon a Seat in a Yew-Tree," Wordsworth had sketched a similar recluse. "The man whose eye / Is ever on himself," he cautions us, "doth look on one / The least of Nature's works ... ." Though the "beautiful abyss" in which the Solitary dwells is a kind of Grasmere, "Not melancholy—no, for it is green, / And bright, and fertile, furnished in itself / With the few needful things that life requires" (II.355–57), we also recognize in it features of the spot-syndrome which elicit or express the apocalyptic imagination and explain the poet's fascination with it. Sterner and milder beauties in alternation suggest a biblical or Miltonic reversal:

> Beneath our feet, a little lowly vale,
> A lowly vale, and yet uplifted high
> Among the mountains ....

This high and low, the verbal lingerings, something rising from the abyss, the reversal of an expected or natural order (sound preceding sight), and the further prolepsis of thinking the Solitary dead, indicate in a deeply ordinary way the stirrings in Wordsworth of "Imagination ... That awful Power" even perhaps as he is composing. I need hardly add how many images of engulfment haunt the narrative at this point: we go from the abyss of II.373 to the unfathomable gulf of III.991.

Wordsworth's attitude toward the Solitary and his abode is full of ambivalence. For the Solitary, like himself, is a new Jonah, who escapes into the deeps of nature. What would he escape from? Imagination. It is not possible to think of him as shunning only the face of man. What he really shuns is the face of God, that is to say, his past strength, his dreams, his young intuitions. But solitude, instead of delivering from these as from the world, declares their greatness. He is forced to suffer a vision of glory (II.834 ff.) and remember his own. Describing a terrible moment in his sea-journey to America (it parallels an episode in "The Female Vagrant" and is linked to Wordsworth's experience on Salisbury Plain), the Solitary tells what may happen when a man is left to himself on the desert of the sea

> O, never let the Wretched, if a choice
> Be left him, trust the freight of his distress

To a long voyage on the silent deep!
For, like a plague, will memory break out;
And, in the blank and solitude of things,
Upon his spirit, with a fever's strength,
Will conscience prey.—Feebly must they have felt
Who, in old time, attired with snakes and whips
The vengeful Furies. *Beautiful* regards
Were turned on me .... (III.844–53)

Two stories are linked to the meeting with the Solitary. The first concerns the man whose funeral the visitors unexpectedly see. A type of Cumberland Beggar, he has been adopted by a housewife of those parts, who gives him, in return for small services, food and shelter, "a blind dull nook ... the *kennel* of his rest." One day, while in the mountains, he is surprised by a storm, and when finally discovered by a search party,

We spake—he made reply, but would not stir
At our entreaty; less from want of power
Than apprehension and bewildering thoughts.
(II.824–26)

And, although he seemed to have received no harm, "a silent change / Soon showed itself: he lingered three short weeks; / And from the cottage hath been borne to-day."

Everything suggests that the Old Man died of other than physical causes. He is found within the ruins of a small chapel on the central heights, almost buried in tufts of heath, and snug as a child. Protection from the storm, yes; but the place, the circumstances, his paralysis, and the manner of his passing away, hint at death by vision as well as by water. Perhaps the vision was merely the terror of the elements from which he hid. The result is still that silent or lingering death characteristic of those who are vision-struck, and no longer able to tolerate, after what they have been, their former selves.

If this is so, the fates of the Old Man and of the Solitary are mirror-images. And it becomes something of a probability when we notice a displacement common enough in literature. The vision which the Old Man may have had is experienced by the Solitary as he returns from the search for him. A step suddenly frees the Solitary from the "blind vapour" (the transferred epithet used pregnantly here) and reveals a scene analogous to that given from Snowdon. "By earthly nature had the effect been wrought / Upon the dark materials of the storm." He seems to see the glory-seat of God. Its footstool is the little valley in which he dwells. More important than the substance of the vision is its effect on the Solitary:

> my heart
> Swelled in my breast.—"I have been dead," I cried,
> "And now I live! Oh! wherefore *do* I live?"
> And with that pang I prayed to be no more! (II.874–77)

It does not matter whether the Old Man had the identical experience. The episode establishes without doubt in what way vision, or Imagination, is death-dealing. From that height the Solitary must descend. Thenceforth his life is death-in-life. He has not escaped the face of God.

The second story, covering the latter half of Book III, is of the Solitary's past. Much of it reflects Wordsworth's own experience, already broached in the eleventh book of *The Prelude*, but remaining unpublished. The part that is new incorporates the poet's loss of his two children in 1812, and was added to *The Excursion* shortly after that.

The Solitary, according to his story, is happily married for seven years, and his thoughts and wishes are finally "bounded" to this world when his children die, and his wife, like Margaret, sinks into a curious inertia:

> Calm as a frozen lake when ruthless winds
> Blow fiercely, agitating earth and sky. (III.650–51)

She, as it were, unbinds herself from the earth, and becomes so aloof even from her husband that he confesses:

> The eminence whereon her spirit stood,
> Mine was unable to attain. (III.659–60)

In a variant, the Solitary calls her "an untranslated spirit." Yet she soon loses that exaltation and wastes away silently:

Dimness o'er this clear luminary crept
Insensibly;—the immortal and divine
Yielded to mortal reflux; her pure glory,
As from the pinnacle of worldly state
Wretched ambition drops astounded, fell
Into a gulf obscure of silent grief,
And keen heart-anguish—of itself ashamed,
Yet obstinately cherishing itself. (III.670–77)

Her manner of dying, then, is similar to that of the Old Beggar, and its cause is probably related. The woman, after losing her second child, is not sealed up in apathy or stoic response, but in vision. She enters a waking slumber impenetrable to human fears. Her love for the two children cannot be sublimated. It is so intense that only an intensified vision of their continued life has the power to replace them. Her mind is unable to accept the thought of death unless assured of a life superior to what is dead, and hope raises her mind to that imagining. But

'tis a thing impossible to frame
Conceptions equal to the soul's desires;
And the most difficult of tasks to *keep*
Heights which the soul is competent to gain. (IV.136–39)

The sorrow which ensues to consume her is not so much anguish at her children's, death as a consequence of that—the drying up of her soul in the effort of continued ecstasy. Perhaps the idea of personal immortality has been so strongly abetted by scriptural consolation that she cannot pass from the belief in supernatural existence to a faith in other than personal subsistence. The "more than human" is identified by her with the "more human," the Person *eminenter*:

Too, too contracted are these walls of flesh,
This vital warmth too cold, these visual orbs,
Though inconceivably endowed, too dim
For any passion of the soul that leads
To ecstasy; and, all the crooked paths
Of time and change disdaining, takes its course
Along the line of limitless desires. (IV.179–85)

BOOK IV: DESPONDENCY CORRECTED

The tragedies of Margaret, the Solitary, and the Solitary's wife, though the first is triggered by the cruelty of governments, the second affected by both political and personal causes, and the last purely domestic, share similarities that, far outweigh their differences. They are tragedies, first of all, of common life, to which the Pastor can add numerous examples in Books V ff. We do not hear "Of carnal, bloody, and unnatural acts." Nor are the persons that are overthrown distinguished in any way, or noble. They are common clay; and Wordsworth continues the aim of *Lyrical Ballads*, which was to choose incidents and situations from ordinary life, describe them as far as possible in language really used by men, and trace through them the primary laws of our nature. Though he does not really succeed in the matter of language, the first book shows he might have achieved "words / Which speak of nothing more than what we are." And though, after Book I, the tenor of *The Excursion* is diverted by various scruples, which include, principally, a fear of the power of vision that is his very subject, Wordsworth still succeeds in providing the first strong account of imagination as the exalted and tragic part of *every* mind. The appetite for vision, related to the appetite for death, needs a "cure of the ground"; and the onus of arguing that cure, without disparaging the nobility of the disease, falls on the Wanderer.

The despondency the Wanderer seeks to correct is less the opposite of hope than its strongest derivative. As a theological virtue, hope was distinguished from faith and love; but the distinction was always somewhat scholastic, and is not operative in Wordsworth. When the Wanderer says that we live by admiration, hope, and love, he is not significantly substituting one virtue for another, but hinting at a psychological scale that proceeds from feelings of awe to gentler sympathies. Wordsworth's experiences are divided into two main kinds, which he often qualifies as sterner and milder, separating man from or binding him to this world. Now hope, in Wordsworth's poetry, as in traditional theology, is the middle virtue, which looks beyond this world, yet still seeks its attachments and enjoyments in the here and now. It is represented by Spenser (and the emblem books) as looking heavenward while leaning on anchor or spade. *Agricolas spes alit*, says the motto, which links the Christian thought to a Virgilian theme, and forms a homely proverb not alien to later Romantic laborers in the vineyards of vision. What Wordsworth calls Imagination is, in this perspective, hope recognizing itself as originally or ultimately independent of this world.

Such a recognition, however, is still dependent on a natural process of birth, or coming-to-mind, which brings back the world and makes hope reflexive. Hope, in fact, is never experienced in a purely unmediated way: the very term imagination is significant in pointing out that hoping is not without images. But no image can ultimately satisfy, and this produces a continual tension. For where nature is too strongly present, hope is not, as St. Paul indicates in a famous definition (Hebrews 11:1). Though Margaret's hope is still attached to this world, that it should be attached at only one point is dangerous: it lives at the expense of everything else. None of Wordsworth's visionaries escapes this monism; their imagination clings to the world by a single (usually human) bond, and seems to prefer death to diminution.

The Wanderer's most powerful argument against visionary despair is also the most Romantic, and is directed less against despair than toward the expansion of hope. The desires should be multiplied. The faculties in man should be multiplied. He who feels contempt for any living thing, Wordsworth says in one of his first poems, has faculties which he has never used; thought with him is in its infancy. (Traherne, in his *Centuries of Meditations*, urges similarly a "sowing of needs.") The eye should not dominate the faculties and man should not be the sole center of our affections. All nature waits to rouse the sleeping energies of the spirit. Let us rise, says the Wanderer, pleading for a reappropriation of this world tantamount to resurrection,

> From this oblivious sleep, these fretful dreams
> Of feverish nothingness. Thus disciplined
> All things shall live in us and we shall live
> In all things that surround us. This I deem
> Our tendency, and thus shall every day
> Enlarge our sphere of pleasure and of pain.

Though repetitious and verbose, the Wanderer's harangue is also affecting because of that. Its rhythm is that of the divided mind which seeks unity of being yet draws its energies from self-division. We feel its turns and counterturns generating a prophetic passion. Blake, also insisting on the liberation of the senses for the sake of expanded perception, would never have used dichotomies this way, at least not common dichotomies. He attempts to stand beyond "fitting and fitted." But if Wordsworth distinguished, as between imagination and nature, senses and intellect, it is not

> That we should pore, and dwindle as we pore,
> For ever dimly pore on things minute,
> On solitary objects, still beheld
> In disconnection dead and spiritless,
> And still dividing and dividing still,
> Break down all grandeur ...

but rather that we should learn, through the very momentum of such speech, the temper of a mind that could dedicate itself either to "one" thing in disconnection, or allow its divided powers to generate, by meditation, new broadsides of the spirit.

But the ultimate argument against visionary despair is the example the Wanderer sets. His attention to the *turnings* of thought and his respect for *vital accidents*, are Wordsworth's own and save this poetry from abstraction. The courage to go out, to take consolation from nature, or to multiply, by an attention to nature, the "spiritual presences of absent things," is not only an argument but has behind it the "strange discipline" of a lifetime. It shows the habit of perfection. The poet's greatness is revealed when his wisdom teeters on the axis of a moment, on a sudden turn of thought, as in the apostrophe to Imagination in the sixth book of *The Prelude*, or here, after he has heard the tale of Margaret:

> my heart
> Went back into the tale which he had told,
> And when at last returning from my mind
> I looked around, the cottage and the elms,
> The road, the pathway, and the garden wall
> Which old and loose and mossy o'er the road
> Hung bellying, all appeared, I know not how
> But to some eye within me all appeared
> Colours and forms of a strange discipline.

> The trouble which they sent into my thought
> Was sweet, I looked and looked again ...

The inward-turning mind could lose itself; it tends toward a visionary image, and we feel strongly the "fixative" urge. But subtly, and as if by a sleight of thought, the normality of the scene prevails, the mind allows nature's calm to blend with its trouble, and lightens into an image of paradise:

> The very sunshine spread upon the dust
> Is beautiful.

Perhaps repose is too quickly achieved, but the preceding fluctuation has shown how precious our mental balance is, and how precarious.

It is all the more puzzling, therefore, to find the Wanderer in Book IV arguing ex cathedra, and mixing the most original with the most commonplace thoughts. When he says, for example,

> Happy is he who lives to understand,
> Not human nature only, but explores
> All natures,—to the end that he may find
> The law that governs each; and where begins
> The union, the partition where, that makes
> Kind and degree, among all visible Beings;
> The constitutions, powers, and faculties,
> Which they inherit,—cannot step beyond,—
> And cannot fall beneath; that do assign
> To every class its station and its office,
> Through all the mighty commonwealth of things;
> Up from the creeping plant to sovereign Man ...
> (IV.332–43)

an idea expressed also in other poems is blended here not only with a Virgilian topos (apt enough) but also with the concept of the Chain of Being, which is superfluous. Yet I cannot believe that it is a mere indigestion of ideas that prompts Wordsworth to this. Perhaps he meant to appropriate to his purpose certain great commonplaces, because they also nourished Milton, his nearest example of the philosophic poet, and

Spenser, and Shakespeare. Wordsworth is a poet even to his faults, though Coleridge's urgings that he should compose the "first and truly philosophical poem" are doubtless responsible for some of the weightiness in Book IV and after.

A few of the more important examples of this admixture of original thought with poetically consecrated notions should be given, both to redeem somewhat the latter stretches of *The Excursion*, and to localize their weakness.

> One adequate support
> For the calamities of mortal life
> Exists—one only ... (IV.10–12)

begins the Wanderer's correction of despondency, yet his *one* is really *many*. Wordsworth stresses the One, which is absolute trust in a providence that converts all accidents to good, because, as in Spenser, the enemy to Hope is Mutability (cf. *Excursion* III.124 ff., 458). At the same time, and almost without transition, other traditional supports against despair are invoked. We meet the argument from design:

> How beautiful this dome of sky;
> And the vast hills, in fluctuation fixed
> At thy command, how awfull Shall the Soul,
> Human and rational, report of thee
> Even less than these! (IV.34–38)

This goes back to Romans 1:19 and Psalm 19. "In fluctuation fixed" is a rather beautiful argument in a minor mode against the power of mutability. There follows a reference to Duty, conceived in stoic terms as a moral vigor not subject to the storms of circumstance (69–73); also a eulogy of ideal or geometric forms, "Whose kingdom is, where time and space are not" (76); and this flows into an address to the deity as the self-sustaining support of all the Chain of Being (79–99). But everything then issues in the apparently contrary affirmation that the world shall pass away, with a further dark foreseeing that the poet's own sight will fail, though this is delicately redressed by a Miltonic note of fortitude:

> Ah! if the time must come, in which my feet
> No more shall stray where meditation leads,

By flowing stream, through wood, or craggy wild,
Loved haunts like these; the unimprisoned Mind
May yet have scope to range among her own,
Her thoughts, her images, her high desires. (IV.103–08)

Such a personal and moody digest of ideas should deny to
Wordsworth the Coleridgean title of *spectator ab extra*. Nor is there,
except for the secret championship of the many against the one, real
philosophical distinction in the ideas offered us. *The Excursion* becomes
increasingly a Romantic commonplace book; and used as such may
afford some enjoyment. Wordsworth himself seems to admit the
desultory yet comprehensive character of his long poem. At one point he
thinks of subtitling his work "views of Nature, Man, and Society." Some
passages, in fact, like his defense of myth and superstition, which begins

Yet rather would I instantly decline
To the traditionary sympathies
Of a most rustic ignorance and take
A fearful apprehension from the owl
Or death-watch: and as readily rejoice,
If two auspicious magpies crossed my way;—
To this would rather bend than see and hear
The repetitions wearisome of sense,
Where soul is dead, and feeling hath no place (IV.613–21)

became quickly the source of a Romantic *topos*, leading perhaps to
Carlyle's words on mythology in "On Heroes and Hero-Worship" and
certainly influencing Keats and Shelley. Ruskin also felt their power.

It must be said, however, that the structure of Book IV is quite
firm, and in one sense important. Wordsworth divides despondency into
two kinds. The first kind is something universal and philosophical, and
everyone knows it who has been haunted by the phantom of mutability.
But the greater part of the book addresses itself to a more particular
despair arising from "loss of confidence in social man" (IV.261). This
was felt by Wordsworth and Coleridge to be the characteristic
melancholy of their time, political in nature, and following on Britain's
betrayal of the French Revolution as well as on the latter's self-betrayal.
The solitary had, in fact, recovered from his grave personal disasters,

risen once more on the wave of hope, and again bound himself to the world during the period of enthusiasm for the Revolution. "Thus was I reconverted to the world; / Society became my glittering bride, / And airy hopes my children" (III.734–36). The metaphor recalls that marriage of mind and nature, of imagination and this world, which Wordsworth urges throughout, but here the Solitary uses it bitterly, knowing the failure of this second marriage.

The Wanderer's concern is primarily with men alienated from politics (in the largest sense of the word) by the events of his time. The Wanderer knows their dejection because he has shared it. He is the Wordsworth who has come through. The "gentle shocks" of nature, according to him, weaned his pride in revolutionary activities and returned him to gradualism. His counsel to the Solitary, therefore, is not simply, leave your solitude and return to the bosom of mankind, but, "A piteous lot it were to flee from Man— / Yet not rejoice in Nature" (IV.575–76).

There is no need to dwell on the particular persuasions used by Wordsworth's spokesman to restore the Solitary's faith in nature, i.e. in nature's power to regenerate the soul. Many are traditional, deriving from the debate between the active and the contemplative life. They place the emphasis less on the one than on the manifold. Take away this or that strength, remove this or that gift, the bounty in nature and the answering vigor of the soul are still infinite. The main line of argument adds little new to the drift of *The Prelude*. He who has dwelt with nature in the past may dwell with her again, and recover his feelings if he trusts himself abroad. Impulses cannot but come to him from the external world; it is up to the individual to have the imaginative power to value them, rather than letting reason, opinion, or a routine self-centeredness limit his "imaginative Will" (IV.1128). Most of these thoughts, which stress the great and fruitful principle of reciprocity, were actually conceived at Racedown and Alfoxden, in the seminal period of 1795–98.

Books V–IX: Elegies in a Country Churchyard

The question as to whether solitude and nature are regenerative leads into the second part of *The Excursion*. The Solitary's skepticism is undaunted. Neither nature nor the rites of the church can really alter, according to him, a man's destiny or purify his heart. The Wanderer brings him to a place where nature and religion seem to join their forces, to the Churchyard among the Mountains. To no avail: in one of his most passionate statements, the Solitary conjures up a Homeric opening of Hades that would destroy all this cant about green graves and rustic virtues:

> If this mute earth
> Of what it holds could speak, and every grave
> Were as a volume, shut, yet capable
> Of yielding its contents to eye and ear,
> We should recoil, stricken with sorrow and shame,
> To see disclosed, by such dread proof, how ill
> That which is done accords with what is known
> To reason, and by conscience is enjoined. (V.250–57)

He insists that rustic loneliness breeds, except in a few rare natures, "selfishness, and cruelty, and vice; / Or, if it breed not, hath not power to cure" (V.889–90).

This gives the challenge direct to the Wanderer, who falls back on the revered support of the Pastor of this mountain village; and the greater portion of what remains of *The Excursion* consists in the Pastor's attempt at rebuttal. Standing in the churchyard, he resurrects in a series of "living epitaphs" the memory of the sufferings and triumphs of his dead parishioners. It is heaping up of exempla in the medieval manner.

Yet many portraits from among this gallery of the dead are deeply moving. Anguish and pain are by no means slighted: this is clearly the poet of *Lyrical Ballads* changing into a pseudo-narrative mode. It is easy, of course, to prefer the company of living rogues to that of dead sufferers. Yet what Blake said of Chaucer's pilgrims, that they are "the Characters which compose all Ages and Nations" and that though some of the names or titles are altered by time, "the Characters themselves for ever remain unaltered, and consequently they are the Physiognomies or Lineaments of Universal Human Life, beyond which Nature never steps," is also applicable to Wordsworth's solitaries. The avaricious matron (VI.675–770), the deaf man, a unique portrait in literature (VII.395–481), the patient woman (VI.906–1052), and the prospector kept alive by "The darksome centre of a constant hope" (VI.212–54), remind us that if suffering is infinite, its types are recurrent.

Those famous misreaders of Wordsworth who say he advocates rural nature as a panacea should be condemned to read *The Excursion* once a day. It might not raise their estimate of the poem, but it would certainly be fit punishment. Nowhere does Wordsworth acknowledge more explicitly the difficulty in reforming human nature. The Pastor cannot even answer the Solitary in a very direct way. Instead of stating roundly that country life restores the soul to health, he argues negatively that it at least is not deleterious to greatness. Native grandeur of soul is present in lowliest as well as highest, and even the "perverseness of a selfish course" can exemplify it. Perverseness is perseverance of a kind, the product of a too rigid hope. But this almost irrelevant and commonplace point hides a deeper intention. The Pastor's first speech had already cautioned against a speculative or proudly objective standpoint vis-à-vis man. Angels, he says, taking up an old theme, see the object as it is, but we are what we see, and try vainly to distance ourselves from ourselves. It is impossible to judge men by the separated reason alone. Love, admiration, fear, desire and hate, these are our organs; without them we are blind. Why should we read the forms of things with an unworthy eye? the Wanderer had asked in Book I. By showing that behind the most selfish course there is a perverted hope or a darkened imagination, the Pastor rebukes the eye of the Solitary. He confirms by the authority of his office, and by invoking scripture, the very vision of things radiating naturally from the Wanderer during his story of Margaret. Again the emphasis of *The Excursion* is put strongly not on argument but on how to acquire "The inward principle that gives effect / To outward argument" (V.572–73).

It may still be doubted whether the latter part of *The Excursion* adds anything essential to what the first books so sufficiently convey. The poet himself acknowledges that the Wanderer had already declared "by what exercise / From visible nature, or the inner self / Power may be trained, and renovation brought" (V.583–85). It is as difficult to defend Books V–IX as to justify their length. They seem to serve Wordsworth as a frame for pictures of humble men and a humble life, and as a repository for homeless passages from the fertile period of 1797–1800.

Only one intention of the poet's casts a glimmer of favor on these books. Though mazy and polemically inefficient, they do answer the Solitary in a curious way. For *The Excursion*, viewed as a whole, or progressively, shows that man stands in communion not only with the living but also with the dead. Behind its conventional religiosity is this more archaic feature. From the beginning, the Wanderer's glance uncovers the truth of the dead and the evidence of the invisible, and the Pastor perfects this spiritual *katabasis* or resurrection by story of the dead. Both open the grave to intensify our vision of the coils of mortality. We are taught to look uninjured on death, vice, and selfishness, which are shown to be the estranged products of a love "all hoping and expecting all" (VII.848, I Corinthians 13:7); a love asking of imagination more than earth can give.

> The riddle Nature could not prove
> Was nothing else but secret love,

writes Clare in his madness; and against this heroism of the soul, which becomes an avarice of the past or of the impossible, the poet sets the expanded eyes of Pastor and Wanderer.

But the realm of the dead is greater than that of the human dead, extending to everything apparently inanimate. The "universe of death," as Wordsworth calls it, borrowing a Miltonic phrase for Hell, includes whatever is barren to mind. "Where man is not, nature is barren," says Blake; and Wordsworth, at about the same time, declares: "All things shall speak of Man." By this he does not mean an extension of the anthropomorphic viewpoint, or even, as in Blake, an infinite expansion of the concept of Man, It might have been better to say, "All things shall speak to Man." Only by such converse can the naked spirit be clothed, the burden of existence become fruitful, and the rape of vision cease. Wordsworth does not insist on Blake's *All* ("More, More, is the cry of the deluded spirit. Nothing but All can satisfy Man") but rather on the *Any*. The Wanderer's final oration evokes a world from which solitude, though not individuality, has been removed, because each thing has the capacity to communicate its being, to "go out":

> All beings have their properties which spread
> Beyond themselves, a power by which they make
> Some other being conscious of their life,
> Spirit that knows no insulated spot,
> No chasm, no solitude; from link to link
> It circulates, the Soul of all the worlds.

This is not only a noble description of the Chain of Being envisioned at its fullest and most dynamic, but also a final cast at the Solitary. The solitary: is he not happier than he knows, less solitary than he knows? He is still a link in the chain that binds living and dead as one company. Who is to say what is living, what is dead, what is nature, what is imagination? Each link may be a life or the source of renovation. Yet the Wanderer never blurs all things as one. By genial enumeration

> There is an active principle alive
> In all things, in all natures, in the flowers
> And in the trees, in every pebbly stone
> That paves the brooks, the stationary rocks,
> The moving waters, and the invisible air ...

—he multiplies the locus as well as the sentiment of life. The individual being is respected. Though Wordsworth appeals to the ancient idea of the *anima mundi*, he avoids all other hypostases, and the movement of his verse carries us away from demonic fixities and sublimely vague personifications. Rooted in so generous, so interactive a world, can hope decay? Only, says the Wanderer, if it divorces itself from that world:

> The food of hope
> Is meditated action; robbed of this
> Her sole support, she languishes and dies.
> We perish also; for we live by hope
> And by desire; we see by the glad light
> And breathe the sweet air of futurity;
> And so we live, or else we have no life. (IX.20–26)

This is the real Chain of Being: take the world from hope, and hope dies; take hope from us, and we die. There is no fallacy, for Wordsworth, in calling the light glad, for, even if it is we who are glad, the power to spread beyond ourselves and to make some other being conscious of life, is what distinguishes life from death and from apocalypse. The specter of selfhood-solitude is purged, and imagination circulates rejoicing through infinite arteries of links.

JONATHAN WORDSWORTH

Introduction to William Wordsworth: The Ruined Cottage

Writing to a friend in 1818, Keats claimed that Wordsworth was a greater poet even than Milton, because he 'thinks into the human heart'.[1] One of the poems that he must certainly have had in mind is *The Ruined Cottage*, published in 1814 as Book I of *The Excursion*, but first written in 1797–8 as an independent work. With *The Brothers* and *Michael*, both of 1800, *The Ruined Cottage* forms a closely knit group of tragic poems that are central to Wordsworth's poetry of the human heart. As a result of being incorporated in a longer work, rather than published separately, *The Ruined Cottage* has been comparatively little known.[2] In 1969, however, it was printed from a manuscript of 1799 preserved at the Wordsworth Library in Grasmere, and it is now firmly established as a great poem in its own right. It is presented below for the first time in a fully annotated and readily available edition.[3] *The Brothers* and *Michael* were published by Wordsworth himself within months of their composition; they are presented here in the text of *Lyrical Ballads* 1800, but with annotation derived from the manuscripts. Punctuation in all three texts is editorial.

The three poems in this volume have it in common that they are about love, and about the feelings of the survivor in a broken relationship. Margaret loses her husband, Leonard his brother, Michael his only son. Wordsworth draws our attention to their suffering not because he is morbidly interested in pain, but because, like Shakespeare,

From *William Wordsworth*. © 1995 by Jonathan Wordsworth.

he sees it as capable of bringing out the deepest and noblest, human emotions. 'Action', he writes in his play, *The Borderers* (1796–7),

> is transitory—a step, a blow,
> The motion of a muscle this way or that ...

Suffering, by contrast,

> is permanent, obscure and dark,
> And has the nature of infinity.
> (*Borderers*, III. v. 60–5)

They are strange words to choose, but they tell us a lot about the poet and his beliefs. Actions, incidents, exciting events, have no place in his work—they themselves are too soon over, and so is the pleasure they stir in the reader. Suffering is different: it does not just happen, it goes on. It is 'obscure and dark' because it cannot be defined, or comprehended; and it 'has the nature of infinity' because it possesses the quality that Wordsworth valued above all, of seeming no longer to be bounded by the limits of ordinary existence.

In another sense, of course, ordinariness is what Wordsworth claimed to be writing about. He told Henry Crabb Robinson in 1837 that he wanted to be remembered only

> for the way in which his poems exhibit man in his essentially human character and relations—as child, parent, husband— the qualities which are common to all men, as opposed to those which distinguish one man from another.[4]

But there are no lowest common denominators in Wordsworth's poetry. Hazlitt described him as having 'a levelling muse', yet this is true only in social terms. The Preface to *Lyrical Ballads* makes it clear that Wordsworth chooses ordinary country people as a way of making claims that are not ordinary at all:

> Low and rustic life was generally chosen because in that situation the essential passions of the heart find a better soil ... are less under restraint, and speak a plainer and more emphatic language.

The qualities that 'all men have in common' are not those which are usually seen in our behaviour 'as child, parent, husband'. They are 'the *essential* passions of the heart', the deep underlying emotions which we are normally least able to show.

To Wordsworth it seemed that the task of the poet was to record these feelings—and to do so in such a way as to make others experience, through the poetry, emotions that were equally 'sane, pure, and permanent'.[5] Read with this in mind, the Preface to *Lyrical Ballads* may be seen as the poet's quest for a permanent language in which to evoke what appeared to him essential, and therefore unchanging, in human emotion.[6] Perhaps few people would now agree that 'Poetry is the first and last of all knowledge ... as immortal as the heart of man' (Preface to *Lyrical Ballads*); but for those who have any degree of sympathy for what Wordsworth was trying to say, *The Ruined Cottage*, *The Brothers* and *Michael* will be very important poems. Each shows him truly thinking into the heart, exploring with a profound tragic intuition what is 'immortal', infinite, in the suffering and hope of an individual human being.

It is important to notice that for the reader of these poems, optimism is made impossible. We are asked to share the 'torturing hope' of the central characters' but we have before us from the first the evidence that hope was pointless. In the case of *The Ruined Cottage*, Wordsworth seems not on have begun with the tragic outcome of his story in mind, but actually to have started writing at the end. Among the first sequences to be composed is his conclusion, describing the final years and death of the heroine:

> '[On this old bench
> For hours she sate, and evermore] her eye
> Was busy in the distance, shaping things
> That made her heart beat quick. Seest thou that path?—
> The green-sward now has broken its grey line—
> There to and fro she paced through many a day
> Of the warm summer, from a belt of flax
> That girt her waist, spinning the long-drawn thread
> With backward steps. Yet ever as there passed
> A man whose garments shewed the soldier's red,
> Or crippled mendicant in sailor's garb,
> The little child who sat to turn the wheel
> Ceased from his toil, and she, with faltering voice,

Expecting still to hear her husband's fate,
Made many a fond inquiry; and when they
Whose presence gave no comfort were gone by,
Her heart was still more sad. And by yon gate
That bars the traveller's road she often sat,
And when a stranger-horseman came, the latch
Would lift, and in his face look wistfully,
Most happy if from aught discovered there
Of tender feeling she might dare repeat
The same sad question.
                    Meanwhile her poor hut
Sunk to decay; for he was gone, whose hand
At the first nippings of October frost
Closed up each chink, and with fresh bands of straw
Chequered the green-grown thatch. And so she sat
Through the long winter, reckless and alone,
Till this reft house, by frost, and thaw, and rain,
Was sapped; and when she slept, the nightly damps
Did chill her breast, and in the stormy day
Her tattered clothes were ruffled by the wind
Even at the side of her own fire. Yet still
She loved this wretched spot, nor would for worlds
Have parted hence; and still that length of road,
And this rude bench, one torturing hope endeared,
Fast rooted at her heart. And, stranger, here
In sickness she remained, and here she died,
Last human tenant of these ruined walls.'[7]

The ruined walls, 'tenanted' now only by animals,[8] belong presumably to an actual cottage that Wordsworth and his sister Dorothy found near Racedown, in Dorset, where they were living in the early summer of 1797. Margaret, however, has a literary source: the brief vignette of a war-widow in Book VII of Southey's *Joan of Arc*, published the previous year. 'Yet did he leave behind', Southey had written of a soldier dying on the battlefield,

One who did never say her daily prayers
Of him forgetful; who to every tale

> Of the distant war lending an eager ear,
> Grew pale and trembled. At her cottage door
> The wretched one shall sit, and with dim eye
> Gaze o'er the plain, where on his parting steps
> Her last look hung.

'Nor ever shall she know', Southey adds,

> Her husband dead, but tortured with vain hope
> Gaze on—then, heart-sick, turn to her poor babe,
> And weep it fatherless.[9]

It must have been a common enough situation when Southey and Wordsworth were writing. The war with France had led to new taxes that fell especially on the poor, and a bad harvest in 1794 had pushed up the price of bread. Men had either enlisted, as Robert does in *The Ruined Cottage*, for the sake of the bounty, or been taken forcibly by the press-gang; and their wives would often not have known whether they were alive or dead. It is very much the material that Wordsworth had used in his own anti-war poem, *Salisbury Plain* (1793–5), and he accepts the story that is hinted at in Southey's lines without feeling the need to make significant changes. The major difference is one of attitude. Southey is making a political protest, but for Wordsworth the war is now almost irrelevant. *The Ruined Cottage* as he points out (rather priggishly) is 'a common tale / By moving accidents uncharactered'—a tale that is 'scarcely palpable / To him who does not think' (ll. 231–6). All the emphasis is on Margaret's states of mind, none on the plot. Those who are willing to think patiently 'into the human heart' will find the poetry full of beauty and power; those who are looking for a good story in a more obvious sense may well be disappointed.

Half-way through his account of the war-widow, Southey moves uncomfortably into the future tense ('At her cottage-door / The wretched one *shall* sit')—pathos is to be extracted from the fact that the woman's suffering is not yet over. Wordsworth instead puts his story firmly in the past, drawing on our sympathy for the dead, and introducing a new immediacy in the contrasts of past and present. The Pedlar who tells the story and the Poet who is his audience sit on the very cottage-bench where Margaret sat 'shaping things / Which made her heart beat quick'—the bench that had been endeared to her by the torturing hope of Robert's return. The desolation around them is the final stage of the story that is being told. We come to know Margaret through her surroundings. So much so, that in the description of her last years she seems almost to be merged with the cottage that is the visible symbol of her decline:

> 'Meanwhile her poor hut
> Sunk to decay; for he was gone, whose hand
> At the first nippings of October frost
> Closed up each chink, and with fresh bands of straw
> Chequered the green-grown thatch. And so she lived
> Through the long winter, reckless and alone,
> Till this reft house, by frost, and thaw, and rain,
> Was sapped; and when she slept, the nightly damps
> Did chill her breast ...'
>   (ll. 476–84)

It is the cottage that sinks to decay, the cottage that is 'poor' and 'reft' (deprived), and missing Robert's attentions.

Of course, as one reads, sympathy is transferred from the cottage to Margaret, to whom it properly belongs. But when he goes on (or back) to write the beginning of his poem, Wordsworth carries with him this curiously strong sense of the cottage itself as having suffered. The Poet as he toils across the 'bare wide common' in the opening lines finds not an ordinary ruin, but 'four naked walls / That stared upon each other' (ll. 31–2). And the same emphasis on the cottage's painful vulnerability is apparent in the Pedlar's formal lament for Margaret:

> 'She is dead,
> The worm is on her cheek, and this poor hut,
> Stripped of its outward garb of houshold flowers,
> Of rose and sweetbriar, offers to the wind
> A cold bare wall whose earthy top is tricked
> With weeds and the rank speargrass.'
>   (ll. 103–8)

The detail of the worm on Margaret's cheek is shockingly physical. Death is felt as a kind of sexual intrusion, and the poet's horror finds expression in his sense of the cottage as brutally stripped, and offering itself (almost it seems in a form of prostitution) to the wind.

In this reading, the weeds and speargrass seem a kind of tawdry finery in which the cottage decks itself, now that its decent original 'garb of houshold flowers' has been stripped away. But there are other ways of looking at Nature's 'silent overgrowings', and at the relation of Margaret to her surroundings. The Pedlar (who unobtrusively guides our reading, as he guides the Poet in his response) draws attention especially to a bond that has existed between Margaret's family and the waters of the well:

> 'Beside yon spring I stood,
> And eyed its waters till we seemed to feel
> One sadness, they and I. For them a bond
> Of brotherhood is broken: time has been
> When every day the touch of human hand
> Disturbed their stillness, and they ministered
> To human comfort. When I stooped to drink
> A spider's web hung to the water's edge,
> And on the wet and slimy foot-stone lay
> The useless fragment of a wooden bowl.'
>   (ll. 82–91)

The last lines sound so ordinary that one might not recognize the pitcher broken at the fountain in Ecclesiastes, but there can be no doubt that Wordsworth had in mind this archetypal image of life stopped at its source.[10] In *An Evening Walk*, published in 1793, he had made a far less subtle allusion

> For Hope's deserted well why wistful look?—
> Choked is the pathway, and the pitcher broke.
>   (ll. 255–6)

In *The Ruined Cottage* stilted metaphors have been replaced by a poetry of everyday life. The deserted well of Hope becomes a real well, the biblical pitcher is now the fragment of a drinking bowl used by Margaret and her family, and the choking of the pathway too becomes an observable detail: 'Seest thou that path? / The green-sward now has broken its grey line' (ll. 457–8). But this movement away from the literary and artificial does not mean that the poetry is no longer symbolic; it means that it is no longer obviously so. Wordsworth has found a way of giving symbols strength by taking them back to their ordinariness. More surprisingly he has also found a way of giving them life.

The bond between the waters of the well and Margaret's family comes, as the poem progresses, to be seen as part of a more general relationship between man and the natural forces amongst which he lives. There is a balance to be preserved. Nature is active, and will 'minister to human comfort' only as long as it is met by countering activity. Because the story begins at the end, we are first aware of the balance—in the symbol of the bowl, and the desolation of the garden—as having completely broken down. Then, as the Pedlar goes back to record the different stages of Margaret's decline, it becomes clear that Wordsworth has devised a peculiarly sensitive way of registering emotional change, without the crudity of direct narrative ('She felt this—she felt that').

The Ruined Cottage is built up around the four visits of the Pedlar to Margaret after her husband's enlistment; but before moving on to her story Wordsworth offers, as a sort of trailer, a brilliant study of the effects of unemployment on Robert:

> 'his good humour soon
> Became a weight in which no pleasure was,
> And poverty brought on a petted mood
> And a sore temper. Day by day he drooped,
> And he would leave his home, and to the town
> Without an errand would he turn his steps,
> Or wander here and there among the fields.
> One while he would speak lightly of his babes
> And with a cruel tongue; at other times
> He played with them wild freaks of merriment,
> And 'twas a piteous thing to see the looks
> Of the poor innocent children. "Every smile",
> Said Margaret to me here beneath these trees,
> "Made my heart bleed."'
>   (ll. 172–85)

The concept of good humour as a weight, the listlessness and alternation of Robert's moods, and especially the observation that it would be the children's smiles, not their sadness or perplexity, that were most painful—all show the extraordinary psychological insight that is to be found in these poems. And the passage is also beautifully handled from a structural point of view. In the long term it shows the rhythms of Robert's life breaking down under stress, as Margaret's will do later; in terms of an immediate effect, it creates for Margaret a sympathy that will be carried over into the main body of the poem. Most of the passage has not seemed to be about her at all, but in the final poignant moment of dialogue we become aware that she has been present throughout. It is she who has told the Pedlar what 'a piteous thing' it was to see the looks of 'the poor innocent children', she who has watched her husband going to pieces, suffered his petted moods and sore temper. The most important line in the passage is one that appears to be doing no work at all:

> '"Every smile",
> *Said Margaret to me here beneath these trees,*
> "Made my heart bleed."'

Not only does the central line delay, and enhance, the effect of Margaret's statement, it brings home her emotion by reference to the trees that have seen it all, and lasted on. Their age and aloofness show up the littleness of the human lives beneath. And yet—as Wordsworth well understood, human feeling when associated with the permanence of Nature may be felt to take on some of the same abiding quality.[11]

The first of the Pedlar's visits after Robert's enlistment finds Margaret grief-stricken and apparently without hope:

> 'With fervent love, and with a face of grief
> Unutterably helpless, and a look
> That seemed to cling upon me, she enquired
> If I had seen her husband.'
> (ll. 254–7)

She is, however, capable of greater resilience than he is himself (presumably he knows too much about the war), and together they 'build up a pile of better thoughts'. 'It was then the early spring', the Pedlar recalls, 'I left her busy with her garden tools.' It seems a casual recollection, but it isn't. Wordsworth has prepared the way for the accounts of Margaret's garden on which we come to depend in the Pedlar's succeeding visits:

> 'I came this way again
> Towards the wane of summer ...
>   In the shade,
> Where now we sit, I waited her return.
> Her cottage in its outward look appeared
> As chearful as before, in any shew
> Of neatness little changed—but that I thought
> The honeysuckle crowded round the door
> And from the wall hung down in heavier tufts,
> And knots of worthless stonecrop started out
> Along the window's edge, and grew like weeds
> Against the lower panes.'

'I turned aside', the Pedlar adds, 'And strolled, into her garden. It was *changed*' (ll. 298–9, 303–13).

The distinction between cottage and garden is not really as marked in this case as Wordsworth's brief dramatic statement makes it sound. Active Nature that has been crowding unrestrained round Margaret's door has been at work in the garden too:

> 'The unprofitable bindweed spread his bells
> From side to side, and with unwieldy wreaths
> Had dragged the rose from its sustaining wall
> And bent it down to earth. The border tufts,
> Daisy, and thrift, and lowly camomile,
> And thyme, had straggled out into the paths
> Which they were used to deck.'
>   (ll. 314-20)

On one level, of course, one can say that Margaret is unhappy, and so not getting on with her gardening. There can be little doubt, however, that Wordsworth saw the choking of the pathways in symbolic terms; and, in addition, it is surely tempting to see the rose, dragged from its sustaining wall, as an emblem of Margaret herself. As with the wooden bowl at the well, there is a concealed allusion—this time not to the Bible, but to *Paradise Lost*. Eve in Book IX, tending roses on her own after taking leave of Adam, is first described as 'stooping to support / Each flower of slender stalk, whose head ... Hung drooping unsustained', and then referred to quite specifically as herself the 'fairest unsupported flower, / From her best prop so far ... ' (ll. 427–33). Margaret's situation is very different of course. It is no fault of hers that 'her best prop' is so far away, and *The Ruined Cottage* contains no serpents or temptations—but the part played by gardening in the two poems remains curiously similar. In each case it represents happy and useful activity, and in each case it is held to be necessary; and yet in neither poem does it have an economic motive. One would surely expect Margaret's to be a vegetable-garden, but it isn't. The point comes through unexpectedly in Wordsworth's language: the bindweed is regarded as 'unprofitable', but is logically no more so than the rose which it has pulled down; and the reference to 'knots of *worthless* stonecrop' is odder still. The crime the knots have committed is to grow 'like weeds' against the window-panes. But by ordinary standards they *are* weeds. The implication seems to be that if the stonecrop were under control it could be accepted, perhaps even regarded as a flower. To be 'profitable', or 'worthy', is to fit into the total scheme of things—in effect, to be orderly.[12] Flowers that straggle out into paths 'which they were used to deck' are no more acceptable than weeds, because both equally symbolize the breaking down of harmony. As Eve puts it,

> what we by day
> Lop overgrown, or prune, or prop, or bind,
> One night or two with wanton growth derides,
> Tending to wild.
>   (*Paradise Lost*, IX. 209–12)

Because of the Fall, we never know if wildness could really have become a threat in Paradise—it hardly seems likely—but in *The Ruined Cottage* we are aware of it as the state that Margaret's garden reaches *at her death*:

> It was a plot
> Of garden-ground now wild, its matted weeds

Marked with the steps of those whom as they passed,
The gooseberry-trees that shot in long lank slips,
Or currants hanging from their leafless stems
In scanty strings, had tempted to o'erleap
The broken wall.
　　　(ll. 54–60)

On the Pedlar's third visit to the cottage, Margaret herself is 'sad and drooping'; her house bespeaks 'a sleepy hand of negligence'; her child has caught from her the 'trick' (habit) of grief, and sighs among its playthings. And yet such are the expectations that have been set up, that we take it for granted the garden will provide the deeper implications:

　　　　　　'Once again
I turned towards the garden-gate, and saw
More plainly still that poverty and grief
Were now come nearer to her. The earth was hard,
With weeds defaced and knots of withered grass;
No ridges there appeared of clear black mould,
No winter greenness. Of her herbs and flowers
It seemed the better part were gnawed away
Or trampled on the earth.'
　　　(ll. 411–19)

There is no logical way in which a garden that has not been dug could tell us more of poverty and grief than an unhappy child. We accept that it does so because the different levels and suggestions of the poetry are working so powerfully together: Margaret too sad to dig; Margaret failing in her bond, and subject to 'the calm oblivious tendencies / Of Nature' (ll. 504–5) that will finally take over; Margaret suffering because in some curious sense she is her surroundings. The flowers that are gnawed away or trampled to the earth represent in all these ways a stage between the harmless, unpainful, encroachments of the honeysuckle and stonecrop, and the brutal last stripping of the household 'garb'. It is at this point that Wordsworth introduces the moving and beautiful symbol of the appletree, sharpening our awareness of suffering by bringing the merely implied grief into the presence of Margaret's actual pain:

'A chain of straw
Which had been twisted round the tender stem
Of a young appletree, lay at its root;
The bark was nibbled round by truant sheep.
Margaret stood near, her infant in her arms,
And, seeing that my eye was on the tree,
She said, "I fear it will be dead and gone
Ere Robert come again."'
          (ll. 419–26)

Margaret thinks of the tree—indeed thinks of everything—in terms of Robert. We, on the other hand, see it in terms of Margaret herself, who of course we know will be 'dead and gone / Ere Robert come again'. It is the bringing together of these two kinds of response that creates this great moment of tragic poetry. The poem has reached a turning-point. Margaret seems utterly despairing; and yet from now on it is her hope not her suffering that will be stressed, because it is hope, persisting in the face of probability and logic, that has the sharper tragic implication. The account of Margaret's last years dominated by her sad, earnest questioning of travellers, and the increasing decay of her cottage—brings Wordsworth to the place where he had started. The earliest versions of the poem were permitted to end blankly and without any attempt at a final consolation, 'and here she died, / Last human tenant of these ruined walls'. In March 1798, however, Wordsworth decided to add the beautiful reconciling image of the speargrass. 'Enough to sorrow have you given', the Pedlar says, addressing the Poet whose 'impotence of grief' for Margaret we are likely to share,

'The purposes of wisdom ask no more:
Be wise and chearful, and no longer read
The forms of things with an unworthy eye:
She sleeps in the calm earth, and peace is here.
I well remember that those very plumes,
Those weeds, and the high speargrass on that wall,
By mist and silent raindrops silvered o'er,
As once I passed did to my mind convey
So still an image of tranquility,
So calm and still, and looked so beautiful

Amid the uneasy thoughts which filled my mind,
That what we feel of sorrow and despair
From ruin and from change, and all the grief
The passing shews of being leave behind,
Appeared an idle dream that could not live
Where meditation was. I turned away,
And walked along my road in happiness.'
                        (ll. 508–25)

To be asked suddenly to think of Margaret's life as a 'passing *shew* of being' seems terribly harsh, and not everybody will be won over by talk of 'meditation' and 'the purposes of wisdom'. But the poetry does have a compelling tranquillity, and there is a special appropriateness in that consolation is offered in terms of the weeds and flowers that have been used throughout to tell the story. One may if one chooses take the speargrass, 'By mist and silent raindrops silvered o'er', to be another emblem of Margaret herself (like the rose and the appletree); but whether one does or not, it is a comfort to think of her as assimilated into the natural world—a part of the wildness that she was finally unable to check. Nor is the Pedlar's wisdom really so unacceptable. He is shown as making a very personal response to the story as he tells it, and he does not say that he is always capable of thinking dispassionately of human suffering—merely that on one occasion the beauty of the speargrass enabled him to do so.

Numerous small echoes suggest that Wordsworth began *The Brothers* at Christmas 1799 with *The Ruined Cottage* in mind. Because of the dramatic form he has now decided to use, the two poems appear very different; but Margaret's story had of course been told within the framework of a conversation, and for the high points Wordsworth had on several important occasions turned to dialogue. In terms of situation too, *The Brothers* seems more a development than a new beginning. Leonard and 'the homely priest of Ennerdale' meet, as the Poet and Pedlar had done, at a spot that prompts the telling of the story. The difference is that Leonard, instead of being the eventual narrator, is one of the principal characters in the story that he hears: in effect he is Robert returned to find out if Margaret is still alive. Because of this there is an element of suspense that is not present in *The Ruined Cottage*. But it is a very muted kind of suspense. The conversation takes place throughout beside James' grave; what we see is not Leonard discovering the fact of his brother's death, but the alternating moods of grief and self-deluding hope as he brings himself to accept it. In effect Wordsworth has once more begun his story at the end, and it is interesting that as with Margaret's cottage (and Michael's sheepfold), his actual starting-point was a relic from the past that had come to be symbolic of mortality.

On a walking-tour in the Lake District in November 1799, Wordsworth and Coleridge heard of the deaths of Jerome Bowman—who broke his leg near Scale Force, crawled three miles at night on hands and knees, and then died from his injuries—and his unnamed son, who, in the laconic words of Coleridge's notebook, 'broke his neck before this, by falling off a crag'. He was 'supposed', Coleridge goes on, 'to have layed down and slept, but walked in his sleep'; and then he adds the detail that especially appealed to Wordsworth's imagination: 'This was at Proud Knot on the mountain called Pillar up Ennerdale. His pike-staff stuck midway and stayed there till it rotted away.'[13] The courage and physical suffering of the elder Bowman did not seem to Wordsworth to be material for poetry; and the story he devised to incorporate the death of Bowman's son makes nothing of the event in its own right. *The Brothers* is about feelings and relationship, about community and loneliness, and about the different kinds of memorial that the dead may leave behind.

It is the wooden bowl found by the Pedlar at Margaret's well that James' staff most strongly recalls as it moulders half-way down the cliff. The staff, or crook, is an emblem of the shepherd's way of life, just as the bowl had represented Margaret's relationship to an outer world, in her giving of water to passers-by.[14] Both objects now are useless and in decay; but, surviving at the places where their owners died, they have come to be memorials—while they last, and while there is somebody there to recognize them. The Pedlar makes the point in lines that lead up to the discovery of the bowl:

> 'I see around me here
> Things which you cannot see. We die, my friend,
> Nor we alone, but that which each man loved
> And prized in his peculiar nook of earth
> Dies with him, or is changed, and very soon

Even of the good is no memorial left.'
                (ll. 67–72)

Margaret has lived and died in isolation: there seems to be no adjacent village, and she has no bonds with the parish, or the nearby town, to which Robert at one point 'turns his steps' (ll. 175–7). Only the Pedlar remains who can 'see' the past amid the desolation of the present.[15] In this respect the situation in *The Brothers* is entirely different. Wordsworth sets his new poem in an ideal village community, of which the dead are effectively still members. As Leonard puts it to the Priest, 'Your dalesmen, then, do in each other's thoughts / Possess a kind of second life' (ll. 182–3). Gravestones are unnecessary because the dead are talked of by the fireside. Everybody knows who everybody was, and so no one can lack a memorial.

As part of the community, James has been 'the child of all the dale', lovingly supported while he lived, and lovingly remembered. Leonard too had once been part of it—indeed their 'bond of brotherhood' had seemed to typify all that was best in the dalesman's way of life (ll. 245–63)—but on his return after twenty years he is unrecognized, regarded as a tourist and a stranger, and even told his own story. He has of course only to say his name, and the church bells will carry the news of his homecoming from Ennerdale to Egremont. But he doesn't, because there is truly a sense in which he is a stranger, isolated by a depth of feeling that could be met perhaps in a reunion with James, but which cannot be softened down, rendered once again part of a general harmony. His hope has been too great, and his loss cannot be shared or contained. James in him will have a memorial of quite another kind.

We first become aware of the strength of Leonard's feelings in the curious account of his self-delusion over James' grave. He has come to the churchyard because he daren't enquire if his brother is still alive, and he has found the extra grave that tells him plainly of his death. Wordsworth's tones at this point are so bare and flat that they seem to say that the whole story is over. Then there is a change:

> but as he gazed there grew
> Such a confusion in his memory
> That he began to doubt, and he had hopes
> That he had seen this heap of turf before

That it was not another grave, but one
He had forgotten.
        (ll. 83–8)

We should be remembering by now that there had already been an example of what imagination can do aided by emotional need. During his twenty years at sea, Leonard not only heard 'The tones of waterfalls and inland sounds' in the piping of the shrouds (ll. 44–5), but 'would often hang / Over the vessel's side, and gaze and gaze' till in the waves beneath him he

Saw mountains, saw the forms of sheep that grazed
On verdant hills, with dwellings among trees,
And shepherds clad in the same country grey
Which he himself had worn.
        (ll. 51–2, 59–62)

In the churchyard the same abstracted gazing produces a sort of 'calenture' of false hope.[16] Recollecting an occasion during the day when he has in fact misremembered a detail from the past, Leonard becomes so exalted that he imagines 'the rocks, / And the eternal hills themselves, [are] changed' (ll. 95–6). There is a playfulness now in Wordsworth's voice—a sort of tender mockery of the mortal who thinks he can see change amid the permanent forms of Nature—but there is admiration too, for the power of love that is implied in such wilful self-deluding.

There is one part of the landscape in which Leonard is right to see a change. 'Aye, there indeed your memory is a friend', the Priest comments,

That does not play you false. On that tall pike
(It is the loneliest place of all these hills)
There were two springs which bubbled side by side
As if they had been made that they might be
Companions for each other!
        (ll. 135–40)

Memory as a friend; springs as companions; and a few lines earlier Leonard has referred to the dalesman's quiet life in which the 'years make *up one peaceful family'*—*The Brothers* is for Wordsworth unusually rich in figurative writing, and especially important are the images of relationship that reflect on the poet's central theme.[17] 'Ten years back', the Priest continues,

> Close to *those brother fountains*, the huge crag
> Was rent with lightning—one is dead and gone,
> The other, left behind, is flowing still.
> (ll. 140–3)

Not only do we know of Leonard and James as the brothers of the poem's title, we have heard them referred to as 'brother shepherds'; given the Priest's humanizing elegiac language ('one is dead and gone'), we are not likely to miss an allusion in the 'brother fountains' that seem as if they were made to be companions to each other. Less obvious is the way the lines are working in dramatic terms. We know that the dead fountain is James; but for Leonard, the Priest's words, if they are assimilated, must be a source of futile hope. After twenty years the Priest would be likely to think of Leonard as dead; it is James who has been 'left behind', and should be 'flowing still'.

We can't be certain that Wordsworth intended this effect, but *The Brothers* is a carefully made poem, and it seems entirely probable. The Priest, with his self-pleasure and his good heart, is a far more sophisticated creation than the Pedlar. For much of the poem his garrulousness convincingly prevents the fact of James' death emerging, and when Leonard does manage to ask a straight question, he doesn't get an answer:

> LEONARD   It seems these brothers have not lived to be
>   A comfort to each other?
> PRIEST   That they might
>   Live to that end, is what both old and young
>   In this our valley all of us have wished—
>   And what, for my part, I have often prayed.
>   But Leonard ...
> LEONARD   Then James still is left among you?
> PRIEST   'Tis of the elder brother I am speaking.
>   They had an uncle ...
>   (ll. 281–8)

Alongside the tension in the dialogue that comes from Leonard's hope—
or from his need to be allowed to hope—there is the reader's growing
wish for him to tell the Priest who he is. Once or twice it seems that he
may have given himself away by showing more knowledge than a
stranger could have possessed; but in fact of course he can neither be
permitted to reveal himself, nor be unmasked, because without James a
joyful homecoming is unthinkable. And so the poem moves on to its
conclusion, in which Leonard, unable to rejoin the community of the
past, or come to terms with his grief, goes back without hope to the sea.
For him the rocks and the eternal hills have indeed been changed.

The Brothers, however, contains more of consolation than either
The Ruined Cottage or *Michael*. Though he cannot reveal himself to the
Priest, Leonard is allowed to set things straight by letter after he has left
the village, and for the reader it is a very welcome concession. He also
of course outlives the poem, as Margaret and Michael cannot, and the
detail of his being '*now* / A seaman, a grey-headed mariner' (ll. 430–1) to
some extent takes the edge off his grief Most important, though, is the
use that Wordsworth makes of Bowman's staff. James falls from the crag,
is found 'Dead, and with mangled limbs' (l. 378), and duly buried.
Leonard is reassured that his brother has not committed suicide, and the
poet quietly introduces the symbol that had been his starting-point:

> We guess that in his hands he must have had
> His shepherd's staff; for midway in the cliff
> It had been caught, and *there* for many years
> It hung—and mouldered *there*.
> (ll. 399–402)

The tones of the verse, the break that occurs at this point in the poem,
and especially the repetition of the word 'there', bring Margaret's death
vividly to mind:

> 'And *here*, my friend,
> In sickness she remained; and *here* she died,
> Last human tenant of these ruined walls.'

Consciously or otherwise, Wordsworth is patterning himself on the
original ending of *The Ruined Cottage*.[18] But where the naked, staring

walls of Margaret's house bring associations only of pain, the survival of
the staff seems oddly consoling. The Priest may take pleasure in James'
decent burial, but the comfort offered to the rest of us is that the staff
has lasted on, peaceful and undisturbed, until in the fullness of time it
rotted away. In its power to assuage it is closer to the speargrass, 'By mist
and silent raindrops silvered o'er', than it is to the cottage. Visible, and
yet out of reach—midway in the cliff; and midway, in effect, between life
and death—it confers upon James a sort of half-life of the imagination.

Coleridge described *The Ruined Cottage* as 'the finest poem in our
language, comparing it with any of the same or similar length', and
referred to *The Brothers* as 'that model of English pastoral, which I have
never yet read with unclouded eye'.[19] There are ways in which *Michael*
is still more impressive. Once again Wordsworth seems to have started
writing with a particular symbol in mind. 'After dinner', Dorothy
records in her *Journal* on 11 October 1800, 'we walked up Greenhead
Gill in search of a sheepfold.' Clearly it was a particular fold which the
poet had noticed already; and like both the cottage and the staff, it was
in a state of decay. As Wordsworth put it, in some beautiful lines that
were not used in the final poem:

> There is a shapeless crowd of unhewn stones
> That lie together, some in heaps, and some
> In lines, that seem to keep themselves alive
> In the last dotage of a dying form.[20]

Dorothy comments that the sheepfold is 'failing away', and then adds a
detail that seems prophetic of the poem that her brother will write: 'it is
built nearly in the form of a heart unequally divided'.

Like the ruined cottage, the sheepfold makes its appearance at the
very beginning of the poem. Wordsworth's tones in introducing it,
however, are much less relaxed. After his experiment with dialogue he
has returned to direct narrative, and addresses the reader in a rather
hearty version of his own voice:

> If from the public way you turn your steps
> Up the tumultuous brook of Greenhead Gill
> You will suppose that with an upright path
> Your feet must struggle ...

But courage! ...
>   (ll. 1–6)

The magical image of the stones keeping themselves alive in the dying form of the sheepfold perhaps seemed to draw too much attention to itself. Wordsworth at any rate discards it, giving us instead a little nudge about how to read his poem:

> Beside the brook
> There is a straggling heap of unhewn stones;
> And to that place a story appertains,
> Which, *though it be ungarnished with events*,
> Is not unfit, I deem, for the fireside
> Or for the summer shade.
>   (ll. 16–21)

As in *The Ruined Cottage*, Wordsworth is telling us that his is 'a common tale / By moving accidents uncharactered', but he has a new motive now since coming back to live in the Lake District.

In January 1801, Wordsworth sent a copy of the two-volume *Lyrical Ballads* to the Whig Leader of the Opposition in the House of Commons, Charles James Fox, drawing his attention especially to *The Brothers* and *Michael*. 'I have attempted', he writes,

> to draw a picture of the domestic affections as I know they exist amongst a class of men who are now almost confined to the North of England. They are small independent *proprietors* of land, here called 'statesmen'—men of respectable education who daily labour on their own little properties.

'The domestic affections', he continues,

> will always be strong amongst men who live in a country not crowded with population, if these men are placed above poverty. But if they are proprietors of small estates which have descended to them from their ancestors, the power which these affections will acquire amongst such men is

inconceivable by those who have only had an opportunity of
observing hired labourers, farmers, and the manufacturing
poor ... This class of men is rapidly disappearing.
(EY, 314–15)

Wordsworth was in fact trying to do several things at once. He was
making a political point about the virtues of Lake District statesmen
(such as Walter Ewbank of *The Brothers*, and Michael); he was trying in
more general terms 'to shew that men who do not wear fine cloaths can
feel deeply' (*EY*, 315); and he was, as ever, writing a poetry of the human
heart, in which politics and class were finally irrelevant.

Michael, great poem though it is, is very slow to get under way.
Wordsworth is too obviously conscious of his mission. In *The Brothers*
the virtues of the people of Ennerdale had emerged through the
dialogue and the Priest's self-pleasure—*his* parishioners would surely be
willing to reap an acre of their neighbour's corn—but *Michael* has no
Priest, or Pedlar, to take responsibility for the poet's views. The first half
of the poem reads like a celebration of the statesman's way of life. Long
daylight hours on the fells tending to the sheep are supplemented by
night-time work, carding and spinning wool around the lamp which has
given the family its reputation, and the cottage its name—the Evening
Star:

> Early at evening did it burn, and late,
> Surviving comrade of uncounted hours
> Which going by from year to year had found
> And left the couple neither gay perhaps
> Nor chearful, yet with objects and with hopes
> Living a life of eager industry.
> (ll. 119–24)

After the very realistic, and not very attractive, detail of the couple's lack
of cheerfulness, the 'eager industry' sounds false, and a little
condescending. In Donne's phrase, Michael and Isabel are reduced to
'country ants'.[21] There are of course moments of unforced imaginative
poetry in the first part of *Michael*: the descriptions of the hidden valley,
for instance, where 'The mountains have all opened out themselves' (l.
7), and of the shepherd on the fells,

> he had been alone
> Amid the heart of many thousand mists
> That came to him and left him on the heights.
>   (ll. 58–60)

But two lines after this last numinous passage, we hear Wordsworth's voice stridently proclaiming,

> *And grossly that man errs* who should suppose
> That the green valleys, and the streams and rocks,
> Were things indifferent to the shepherd's thoughts.
>   (ll. 62–4)

Wordsworth needed to believe that Michael would be responsive to the natural world about him, because in general he wished to portray the statesman's life as an ideal. But for the purposes of his poem, the green valleys were to be seen, and loved, chiefly as inherited land—a guarantee of the shepherd's independence. The central conflict of the poem was explained by Wordsworth in April 1801 to Thomas Poole, the Somerset farmer who had to some extent been a model for Michael himself:

> In the last poem of my second volume I have attempted to give a picture of a man of strong mind and lively sensibility, agitated by two of the most powerful affections of the human heart: the parental affection, and the love of property, *landed* property, including the feelings of inheritance, home, and personal and family independence.
>   (*EY*, 322)

Unlike *The Ruined Cottage* and *The Brothers*, *Michael* is a tragedy of choice. Margaret and Leonard are blameless in their suffering; Michael to some extent is the cause of his. Because of his age, dignity, and passionate integrity of life, it is difficult to think of him as wrong; but when he says, at the central moment in the poem, 'Heaven forgive me, Luke, / If I judge ill for thee' (ll. 389–90), there can be no doubt that he has done so. Too strongly identified with his land, he has attempted a compromise, when he might—and probably *should*—have responded wholly in terms of his love for Luke. As a result, he loses what is truly most important, and dies in tragic awareness of the mistake that he has made. And yet he has the entire sympathy of the poet, not just in his later suffering, but also in making the wrong decision.

Though isolated and ideal in its different way, the pastoral world of Wordsworth is not protected, as its more literary predecessors had been, from commercial realities. Walter Ewbank and Michael both inherit land that is heavily mortgaged. Walter dies under the burden; Michael pays off his original debt, but then offers a guarantee to his nephew, and suddenly in old age finds that his bond has been called in. His response is dignified and extremely sad:

> 'Isabel', said he,
> Two evenings after he had heard the news,
> 'I have been toiling more than seventy years,
> And in the open sunshine of God's love
> Have we all lived, yet if these fields of ours
> Should pass into a stranger's hand, I think
> That I could not lie quiet in my grave.'
> (ll. 236–42)

The last statement has an almost pedantic carefulness that increases its poignancy: the land, of course, will pass into a stranger's hand, and Michael will have no option but to lie quiet in his grave. Wordsworth catches beautifully too the confusions involved in the moment of wrong decision:

> 'When I began, my purpose was to speak
> Of remedies, and of a chearful hope.
> Our Luke shall leave us, Isabel; the land
> Shall not go from us, and it shall be free
> He shall possess it, free as is the wind
> That passes over it.'
> (ll. 252–7)

Michael's intention is that Luke shall be away only for the time it takes to earn the necessary money; he can then come back to enjoy his inheritance. Through excited rhythms and jumbled trains of thought, however, Wordsworth has been able to suggest that Michael's priorities are far more confused than he knows. Luke's departure is seized on too eagerly as a remedy and cheerful hope, and the parallelism of 'Our Luke shall leave us' / 'The land shall not go from us' is there to suggest what exactly it is that is going wrong. The poetry is saying loudly and clearly that Luke and the land are alternatives. Not recognizing this, Michael temporarily values the land more highly than his son. That is to say, because he thinks he is going to lose it, he not unnaturally gives it more thought than he gives to Luke, in whom he feels secure. That this should matter is tragically unfair, but it does. In some ways Michael's next statement, or clause, is more telling even than the balancing of Luke and land. We expect 'The land shall not go from us' to be followed by 'and Luke will soon come back to enjoy it'; but the line of course continues, 'and it shall be free'. Even when Luke does again become the centre of his father's thoughts, and the subject of his sentence ('*He* shall possess it, free as is the wind / That passes over it'), the adjective 'free', which seems to be his by right, turns out to belong once more to the land. Wordsworth is not merely thinking into the human heart, he is portraying its confusions with extraordinary skill.

The land has been the centre of Michael's life, and of the life of his fathers; properly it should one day be the centre of Luke's. One way of looking at Michael's position is to say that it is in fact possible for him to value Luke above the land, because the two are not in his mind distinct. It is in terms of the land that he values both himself and his son. Luke exists as its next possessor. 'Here they lived', says Michael of his own parents,

> 'As all their forefathers had done; and when
> At length their time was come, they were not loth
> To give their bodies to the family mold.
> I wished that thou should'st live the life they lived;'
> (ll. 376–80)

Luke was born to be the continuation of a line—'thou art the same / That wert a promise to me ere thy birth' (ll. 342–3)—and without the land he could not be so. Michael can scarcely be said to have had a choice. Both his decision and his tragedy seem fated.

We are never told how much Michael himself has understood. Our first information about his feelings comes from Isabel, who has herself inferred it not from anything that Michael says but from his movements in his sleep. One is reminded of the sighs which in *The Ruined Cottage* come on the Pedlar's ear from no apparent source (ll. 385–7). It is a beautiful example of Wordsworth's dealings in implication and indirection, and far more moving than any form of outright statement could have been. But it doesn't of course tell us the nature of Michael's sufferings. Isabel, who (in Wordsworth's rather condescending phrase from *The Prelude*) is 'wise, as women are', assumes that he is grieving straightforwardly over Luke's departure:

> 'Thou must not go,
> We have no other child but thee to lose,
> None to remember—do not go away,
> For if thou leave thy father he will die.'
>   (ll. 304–7)

It is possible, however, to read the signs as implying not merely grief, but anxiety over the decision that has been taken; and in the great central episode of the laying of the corner-stone, we are encouraged to do so.

The final stages of the poem move from the cottage to the sheepfold or to the site of the sheepfold—beside the boisterous brook of Greenhead Ghyll. There Michael, whose impressiveness seems more and more to recall the Old Testament, arranges a formal leave-taking, and binds Luke to a covenant:

> ''tis a long time to look back, my son,
> And see so little gain from sixty years.
> These fields were burthened when they came to me;
> Till I was forty years of age, not more
> Than half of my inheritance was mine.
> I toiled and toiled; God blessed me in my work,
> And till these three weeks past the land was free
> It looks as if it never could endure
> Another master. Heaven forgive me, Luke,
> If I judge ill for thee, but it seems good
> That thou should'st go.'
>   (ll. 381–91)

Earlier, Michael had felt he could not lie quiet in his grave if the land passed into the hand of a stranger; now, as his own emotions become stronger and more confused, the land itself is felt to rebel at the thought. More than half conscious of judging ill for Luke, Michael makes with him a strange bond which seems to be designed above all to assuage his own anxieties:

> 'I will begin again
> With many tasks that were resigned to thee;
> Up to the heights, and in among the storms,
> Will I without thee go again, and do
> All works which I was wont to do alone
> Before I knew thy face ...
>   but I forget
> My purposes. Lay now the corner-stone
> As I requested, and hereafter, Luke,
> When thou art gone away, should evil men
> Be thy companions, let this sheepfold be
> Thy anchor and thy shield. Amid all fear,
> And all temptation, let it be to thee
> An emblem of the life thy fathers lived ...
>   Now, fare thee well.
> When thou return'st, thou in this place wilt see
> A work which is not here. A covenant
> 'Twill be between us—but whatever fate
> Befall thee, I shall love thee to the last,
> And bear thy memory with me to the grave.'
>   (ll. 401–6, 412–19, 421–6)

Ritual is not at all common in Wordsworth's poetry, and it is worth asking what has been achieved by the solemnity of this moment. From Michael's point of view, the covenant is a way of sharing still with Luke in the building of the fold which they had been going to do together— and, by an extension, a means of sharing in the larger task that Luke has been sent to London to accomplish. But it is more than this. A sort of magic is going on—a claiming of Luke. In laying the corner-stone, he dedicates himself to the way of life that his fathers have led. The fold is to be for him what Nature had been for the poet of *Tintern Abbey*, 'the

anchor of [his] purest thoughts'. All this must one feels have
Wordsworth's sympathy; and yet, as an emblem and protection the
sheepfold proves to be useless. We know no details, but Luke clearly
yields to temptation despite the powers it should have had. As in his
original decision, Michael is attempting in the covenant to have things
both ways—to keep Luke, though sending him away—and his magic
cannot be successful. In the parallel that many readers feel between
Michael and Luke, Abraham and Isaac, there may even be a hint of the
ritual turning to sacrifice: Luke sacrificed to his father's gods.

Michael, it may be thought, attempts by the sheepfold to ratify his
own mistake, claiming Luke as a partner in the wrong decision that has
been made, by dedicating him to the very preoccupation that has been
its cause. But not everybody will wish to read the poem in this way.
Looked at from another point of view, the covenant is akin to Margaret's
bond with waters of the well. Michael's stones are not alive like
Margaret's flowers—the most they can do is 'straggle'—and the
sheepfold is not used, as the garden is, to mark progressive stages of
decline. At the end of the poem, however, the fold enables Wordsworth
to form a tragic conclusion that neither *The Ruined Cottage* nor *The
Brothers* can match.

Michael's foreboding words, 'but whatever fate / Befall thee, I shall
love thee to the last', tell the reader what to expect, but not how the poet
is to bring his poem to a climax. In the event, Luke is shuffled off to his
'hiding-place beyond the seas' (l. 456) with rather disgraceful speed,
leaving Wordsworth free to tell us of Michael's final years. 'There is a
comfort in the strength of love', he begins, quietly saying the opposite of
what we should expect,

> 'Twill make a thing endurable which else
> Would break the heart—old Michael found it so.
> I have conversed with more than one who well
> Remember the old man, and what he was
> Years after he had heard this heavy news.
> His bodily frame had been from youth to age
> Of an unusual strength. Among the rocks
> He went, and still looked up upon the sun,
> And listened to the wind, and, as before,
> Performed all kinds of labour for his sheep

And for the land, his small inheritance.
And to that hollow dell from time to time
Did he repair, to build the fold of which
His flock had need.
               (ll. 456–70)

The poetry seems to be telling us again and again that Michael is all right. The strength of his love (which one might have thought would be painful) is felt as a comfort; the loss of Luke (which should have been heart-breaking) is seen merely as an endurable *thing*; eyewitnesses testify to his having lived on for years, not only strong as ever, but also sensitive and industrious; at times, it seems, he was even capable of going to work at the sheepfold. But underneath all this, one feels the *need* for comfort—the resilience that it took to survive the heart-break and to go on living all that time according to the standards of the past. A series of allusions take us back into the poem, and bring out an especial poignancy. The reference to Michael's bodily frame repeats exactly lines 43–4 (except that we didn't know then how the unusual strength would finally be tested). The moving thought that Michael '*still* looked up upon the sun, / And listened to the wind' (refusing to be bowed) has behind it not just the days when he had seemed to live 'in the open sunshine of God's love' (l. 239), and 'learned the meaning of all winds' (l. 48), but a specific allusion to companionship with Luke:

               from the boy there came
Feelings and emanations, *things which were*
Light to the sun and music to the wind ...
               (ll. 210–12)

The lines that follow are packed with implications—Wordsworth nowhere writes with more feeling and control. Michael performing all kinds of labour for his sheep, and for the land, recalls his tender services to the infant Luke (ll. 162–8); and the fact that they are still 'his sheep', and the land is 'his small inheritance' (he is eighty-four), brings the grief of Luke's absence that much closer to the mind. Finally there is 'that hollow dell' to which

            from time to time
[He did] repair, to build the fold of which
His flock had need.

It is the poet's not referring to the covenant that brings it so strongly to the mind (it is neither here nor there whether the flock has need). ''Tis not forgotten yet', Wordsworth continues, at last conceding Michael's ordinary humanity,

    The pity which was then in every heart
    For the old man; and 'tis believed by all
    That many and many a day he thither went,
    And never lifted up a single stone.
                    (ll. 470–4)

Michael will love Luke to the last, and bear his memory with him to the grave, but he cannot finish the sheepfold that was his own part in the covenant. To have completed the building would have been a sort of restitution to Luke—perhaps even a sort of justification for Michael himself. Neither, in this sternly tragic poem, can be permitted. Michael too fails in his bond. It is in his failure, however, that we feel the greatness of his love.

NOTES

1. Keats to John Hamilton Reynolds, 3 May 1818.

2. For a brief outline of the different changes that *The Ruined Cottage* went through before becoming part of *The Excursion*, see Notes, below.

3. For the first publication of *The Ruined Cottage* as a separate work, see Jonathan Wordsworth, *The Music of Humanity* (London and New York, 1969). More recently the poem has been edited by James A. Butler, with full textual apparatus and photographs of the surviving manuscripts, as a volume in the Cornell Wordsworth Series (Ithaca, N.Y., 1979)—'Butler' in future references.

4. *Henry Crabb Robinson on Books and Their Writers*, ed. E.J. Morley (3 vols., London, 1938), II, 535.

5. As well as reflecting faithfully the feelings of human nature, Wordsworth commented to John Wilson in a letter of 7 June 1802, a great poet 'ought to a certain degree to rectify men's feelings ... to render their feelings more sane, pure, and permanent, in short, more consonant to Nature—that is,

to eternal Nature, and the great moving spirit of things', *Letters of William and Dorothy Wordsworth: The Early Years* ('*EY*' in future references), revised by Chester L. Shaver, Oxford, 1967, p. 355.

6. At both the beginning and the end of the Preface, Wordsworth expresses the hope that his critical positions have enabled him to write a kind of poetry 'adapted to interest mankind permanently'.

7. Lines 454–92, quoted in the earliest surviving version, transcribed by Dorothy for Coleridge on 10 June 1797, *Letters of Samuel Taylor Coleridge* ('Griggs' in future references), ed. E.L. Griggs (6 vols., Oxford, 1956-71), I, 327–8.

8.

> the unshod colt,
> The wandering heifer and the potter's ass,
> Find shelter now within the chimney-wall
> Where I have seen her evening hearthstone blaze ...
>   (ll. 111–14)

9. *Joan of Arc*, VII. 320–31. Wordsworth had certainly read Southey's poem, but may also have seen the lines about the war-widow reprinted in Coleridge's periodical, *The Watchman*, 1 March 1796.

10. See the great final chapter of Ecclesiastes, 'Remember now thy Creator in the days of thy youth':

> Or ever the silver cord be loosed, or the
> golden bowl be broken, or the pitcher be broken
> at the fountain, or the wheel broken at the cistern.
>   Then shall the dust return to the earth as it
> was: and the spirit shall return unto God who gave it.

11. Wordsworth himself would go a lot further. He has, he says in the Preface to *Lyrical Ballads*, 'a deep impression of certain inherent and indestructible qualities of the human mind; and likewise of certain powers in the great and permanent objects [of Nature] that act upon it, which are equally inherent and indestructible'.

12. Wordsworth seems later to have become aware of the more usual sense in which a garden could be 'profitable'; in Excursion Book I—the rose pulled from its sustaining walls becomes, by an unconscious pun, 'two small rows of peas'.

13. *Notebooks of Samuel Taylor Coleridge*, ed. Kathleen Coburn (3 vols. so far, New York and London, 1957–) I, entry 540.

14. The importance of Margaret's charity is discussed in *Music of Humanity* (London and New York, 1969), p. 128.

15. To some extent the Poet becomes able to do so too, as a result of listening to the story (*Ruined Cottage*, 501–7).

16. The 'calenture' is correctly a disease of the tropics in which sailors leap overboard in the delusion that they see green fields, but Wordsworth uses it as a sort of mirage at sea. For the source of his description, see Notes, below.

17. In retrospect one may notice, for instance, the pair of combs which at ll. 32–3 the Priest lays 'with gentle care, / Each in the other locked'—as Leonard and James can never be.

18. See Notes, below.

19. Coleridge to Lady Beaumont, 3 April 1815 (Griggs, iv, 564), and *Biographia Literaria*, ed. George Watson (Everyman's Library, London, 1956), chapter XVIII, 217n.

20. *Poetical Works of William Wordsworth*, ed. E. de Selincourt and Helen Darbishire, Oxford, 1940–9 ('*Oxford Wordsworth*' in future references), II, 482; Wordsworth wrote a great deal for *Michael* that was not included in the printed poem. For other memorable passages from the drafts, see notes to ll. 13–17 and 62–4, below.

21. *The Sunne Rising*, 8.

Chronology

1770	William Wordsworth born on April 7 in Cockermouth in Cumberland County, England.
1771	Sister Dorothy Wordsworth born.
1778	Mother, Ann Wordsworth, dies.
1779–1787	Attends Hawkshead grammar school.
1783	Father, John Wordsworth, dies; two uncles become guardians for William and his four brothers and sisters.
1787	Enters St. John's College, Cambridge.
1790	Carries out walking tour in Europe with friend Robert Jones.
1791	Receives bachelor's degree from Cambridge in January; takes walking tour of Wales with Jones; leaves in November for France.
1792	Has relationship with Annette Vallon in France, fathers a child; returns to England in December.
1793	Publishes *An Evening Walk* and *Descriptive Sketches*; walks across Salisbury Plain.
1794	Lives at Windy Brow with Dorothy; begins caring for Raisley Calvert.
1795	Calvert dies, leaving Wordsworth £900; England declares war on France; meets Samuel Taylor Coleridge; settles in Racedown with Dorothy.
1797	Completes *The Borderers*, a verse drama; Coleridge visits Racedown; Wordsworth and Dorothy move to Alfoxden to be near Coleridge.

1798	Publishes *Lyrical Ballads and Other Poems* with Coleridge; goes to Germany with Coleridge, Dorothy, and others.
1799	Returns to England; tours Lake District with Coleridge and Dorothy; settles at Dove Cottage in Grasmere, Westmoreland County; begins work on *The Prelude*.
1802	After death of Lord Lowther, his son agrees to give Wordsworth children the money owed by him to their father; travels to France with Dorothy to meet Vallon and Wordsworth's daughter Caroline; returns to England and marries Mary Hutchinson.
1803	Travels in Scotland with Dorothy and Coleridge.
1805	Brother John drowned in a shipwreck; completes first version of *The Prelude*.
1808	Family moves to Allan Bank.
1810	Break with Coleridge.
1812	Resumes friendship with Coleridge; both daughter Catherine (age four) and son Thomas (age six) die.
1813	Named Distributor of Stamps for Westmoreland county; settles at Rydal Mount in Grasmere.
1814	Tours Scotland with wife and sister-in-law.
1816	Elder brother Richard Wordsworth dies.
1820	Tours Switzerland and northern Italy with wife and Dorothy.
1828	Trip to Holland and Germany with daughter Dorothy and Coleridge.
1831	Dorothy falls seriously ill.
1833	Dorothy ill again; condition deteriorates.
1839	Works in favor of a copyright law protecting authors' rights in their work.
1842	Leaves position as Distributor of Stamps; given pension.
1843	Named Poet Laureate of England.
1847	Daughter Dora dies.
1850	Wordsworth dies on April 23, age 80; *The Prelude* first published.
1855	Sister Dorothy dies.
1859	Wife Mary Hutchinson Wordsworth dies.

Works by William Wordsworth

An Evening Walk, 1793.

Descriptive Sketches, 1793.

Lyrical Ballads and Other Poems (with Samuel Taylor Coleridge), 1798.

Lyrical Ballads, second edition, 1800.

Poems in Two Volumes, 1807.

The Excursion, 1814.

Poems, 1815.

The White Doe of Rylstone, 1815.

Peter Bell, 1819.

The Waggoner, 1819.

Poems, 1820.

The River Duddon, A Series of Sonnets, 1820.

Ecclesiastical Sketches, 1822.

A Description of the Scenery of the Lakes, 1822.

Poetical Works, 1827.

Yarrow Revisited and Other Poems, 1835.

Poems, Chiefly of Early and Late Years, 1842.

Poetical Works, 1849.

The Prelude, 1850.

"The Ruined Cottage," 1949.

"Salisbury Plain," 1975.

Works about William Wordsworth

Abrams, Meyer Howard, ed. *Wordsworth: A Collection of Critical Essays*. Englewood Cliffs, NJ: Prentice-Hall, 1972.

Averill, James H. *Wordsworth and the Poetry of Human Suffering*. Ithaca: Cornell University Press, 1980.

Baker, Jeffrey. *Time and Mind in Wordsworth's Poetry*. Detroit, MI: Wayne State University Press, 1980.

Beer, John Bernard. *Wordsworth and the Human Heart*. New York: Columbia University Press, 1978.

Bialostosky, Don H. *Making Tales: The Poetics of Wordsworth's Narrative Experiments*. Chicago: The University of Chicago Press, 1984.

Bloom, Harold, ed. *William Wordsworth: Comprehensive Research and Study Guide*. Philadelphia: Chelsea House, 1999.

————. *The Visionary Company: A Reading of Romantic Poetry*. Ithaca: Cornell University Press, 1971.

Brett, R. L., and Jones, A. R., eds. *Lyrical Ballads, 1798 and 1800*. London: Methuen, 1978.

Butler, James, ed. *The Ruined Cottage and The Pedlar*. Ithaca: Cornell University Press, 1979.

Butler, Marilyn. *Romantics, Rebels, and Reactionaries: English Literature and Its Background, 1760–1830*. New York: Oxford University Press, 1982.

Byatt, Antonia Susan. *Wordsworth and Coleridge in Their Time*. London: Nelson, 1970.

Coleridge, Samuel Taylor. *Biographia Literaria*. Eds. James Engell and W. Jackson Bate. 2 vols. Princeton: Princeton University Press, 1983.

———. *Coleridge's Poems and Prose.* Selected by Kathleen Raine. London: Penguin, 1957.

———. *Collected Letters of Samuel Taylor Coleridge.* Ed. Earl Leslie Griggs. 6 vols. Oxford: Oxford University Press, 1912.

Curtis, Jared. *The Fenwick Notes of William Wordsworth.* London: Bristol Classical Press, 1993.

Davies, Hunter. *William Wordsworth, A Biography.* London: Weidenfield and Nicolson, 1980.

De Selincourt, Ernest. *The Early Wordsworth.* The English Association Presidential Address, November 1936. Oxford: Oxford University Press, 1936.

Devlin, David Douglas. *Wordsworth and the Poetry of Epitaphs.* London: Macmillan Press, 1980.

———. *Wordsworth and the Art of Prose.* London: Macmillan Press, 1983.

Ferguson, Frances. *Wordsworth: Language as Counter-Spirit.* New Haven: Yale University Press, 1977.

Gérard, Albert S. *English Romantic Poetry: Ethos, Structure, and Symbol in Coleridge, Wordsworth, Shelley, and Keats.* Berkeley: University of California Press, 1968.

Gill, Stephen, ed. *The Salisbury Plain Poems of William Wordsworth.* Ithaca: Cornell University Press, 1975.

———, ed. *William Wordsworth: The Major Works.* New York: Oxford University Press, 2000.

———. *Wordsworth: A Life.* Oxford: Clarendon, 1989.

Grob, Alan. *The Philosophic Mind: A Study of Wordsworth's Poetry and Thought, 1797–1805.* Columbus: Ohio University Press, 1973.

Halliday, F. E. *Wordsworth and His World.* London: Thames and Hudson, 1970.

Hartman, Geoffrey H. *Wordsworth's Poetry.* New Haven: Yale University Press, 1971.

———, ed. *New Perspectives on Coleridge and Wordsworth.* New York: Columbia University Press, 1972.

Havens, Raymond Dexter. *The Mind of a Poet.* Baltimore: Johns Hopkins University Press, 1941.

Hayden, John O., ed. *The Poems of William Wordsworth.* New Haven: Yale University Press, 1981.

Heath, William. *Wordsworth and Coleridge: A Study of Their Literary Relations in 1801–1802.* New York: Oxford University Press, 1970.

Heffernan, James A. W. *William Wordsworth's Theory of Poetry: The Transforming Imagination*. Ithaca: Cornell Univeristy Press, 1969.

Hodgson, John A. *Wordsworth's Philosophical Poetry 1797–1814*. Lincoln: University of Nebraska Press, 1980.

Jackson, Wallace. *The Probable and the Marvelous: Blake, Wordsworth, and the 18th Century Critical Tradition*. Athens: University of Georgia Press, 1978.

Jacobus, Mary. *Tradition and Experiment in Wordsworth's Lyrical Ballads (1798)*. Oxford: Clarendon Press, 1976.

Jaye, Michael C., Jonathan Wordsworth, and Robert Woof. *William Wordsworth and the Age of English Romanticism*. London: Rutgers University Press, 1987.

Johnson, Lee M. *Wordsworth's Metaphysical Verse: Geometry, Nature, and Form*. Toronto: University of Toronto Press, 1982.

Johnston, Kenneth R. *Wordsworth and* The Recluse. New Haven: Yale University Press, 1984.

Jones, A. R., and R. L. Bret, eds. *Lyrical Ballads: Wordsworth and Coleridge*. London: Routledge, 1992.

Jones, Henry John Franklin. *The Egotistical Sublime: A History of Wordsworth's Imagination*. London: Chatto and Windus, 1954.

King, Alexander. *Wordsworth and the Artist's Vision*. London: Athlone Publishers, 1966.

Mahoney, John L. *William Wordsworth: A Poetic Life*. New York: Fordham University Press, 1997.

Mayberry, Tom. *Coleridge and Wordsworth: Crucible of Friendship*. Thrupp, England: Sutton, 2000.

McConnel, Frank D. *The Confessional Imagination: A Reading of Wordsworth's Prelude*. Baltimore: Johns Hopkins University Press, 1974.

McFarland, Thomas. *Romanticism and the Forms of Ruin: Wordsworth, Coleridge, and the Modalities of Fragmentation*. Princeton: Princeton University Press, 1981.

Moorman, Mary. *William Wordsworth: A Biography*. I. *The Early Years: 1770–1803*. Oxford: Clarendon, 1957; II. *The Later Years: 1803–1850*. Oxford: Clarendon, 1965.

Murray, Roger. *Wordsworth's Style, Figures, and Themes in the Lyrical Ballads of 1800*. Lincoln: University of Nebraska Press, 1967.

Onorato, Richard. *The Character of the Poet: Wordsworth in "The Prelude."* Princeton: Princeton University Press, 1971.

Owen, W. J. B., ed. *Wordsworth's Literary Criticism*. London: Routledge and Kegan Paul, 1974.

Owen, W. J. B., and Jayne Worthington Smyser, eds. *The Prose Works of William Wordsworth*. Oxford: Clarendon Press, 1974.

Parrish, Stephen Maxfield. *The Art of the Lyrical Ballads*. Cambridge: Harvard University Press, 1973.

———, ed. *The Prelude, 1798–1799*. Ithaca: Cornell University Press, 1977.

Perkins, David. *The Quest for Permanence: The Symbolism of Wordsworth, Shelley, and Keats*. Cambridge: Harvard University Press, 1959.

———. *Wordsworth and the Poetry of Sincerity*. Cambridge: Belknap Press, 1964.

Pirie, David. *William Wordsworth: The Poetry of Grandeur and of Tenderness*. London: Methuen, 1982.

Purvis, John. *A Preface to Wordsworth*, rev. ed. Harlow, England: Longman, 1986.

Reed, Mark L. *Wordsworth: The Chronology of the Middle Years, 1800–1815*. Cambridge: Harvard University Press, 1975.

Reguerio, Helen. *The Limits of Imagination: Wordsworth, Yeats, and Stevens*. Ithaca: Cornell University Press, 1976.

Rehder, Robert. *Wordsworth and the Beginnings of Modern Poetry*. Totowa, New Jersey: Barnes and Noble, 1981.

Roper, Derek, ed. *Lyrical Ballads, 1805*. London: Collins, 1968.

Sheats, Paul D., ed. *The Poetical Works of Wordsworth*. Boston: Houghton Mifflin, 1982.

Sherry, Charles. *Wordsworth's Poetry of the Imagination*. Oxford: Clarendon Press, 1980.

Simpson, David. *Wordsworth and the Figurings of the Real*. London: Macmillan Press, 1982.

Watson, J. R. *Wordsworth's Vital Soul: The Sacred and the Profane in Wordsworth's Poetry*. London: Macmillan, 1982.

Contributors

HAROLD BLOOM is Sterling Professor of the Humanities at Yale University and Henry W. and Albert A. Berg Professor of English at the New York University Graduate School. He is the author of over 20 books, including *Shelley's Mythmaking* (1959), *The Visionary Company* (1961), *Blake's Apocalypse* (1963), *Yeats* (1970), *A Map of Misreading* (1975), *Kabbalah and Criticism* (1975), *Agon: Toward a Theory of Revisionism* (1982), *The American Religion* (1992), *The Western Canon* (1994), and *Omens of Millennium: The Gnosis of Angels, Dreams, and Resurrection* (1996). *The Anxiety of Influence* (1973) sets forth Professor Bloom's provocative theory of the literary relationships between the great writers and their predecessors. His most recent books include *Shakespeare: The Invention of the Human* (1998), a 1998 National Book Award finalist, *How to Read and Why* (2000), and *Genius: A Mosaic of One Hundred Exemplary Creative Minds* (2002). In 1999, Professor Bloom received the prestigious American Academy of Arts and Letters Gold Medal for Criticism, and in 2002 he received the Catalonia International Prize.

DALE ANDERSON studied English and American literature at Harvard University. He is a freelance writer and editor. His other books include biographies of Saddam Hussein and Maria Mitchell.

NEIL HEIMS is a freelance writer, editor and researcher. He has a Ph.D. in English from the City University of New York.

GEOFFREY H. HARTMAN is Sterling Professor Emeritus of English and Contemporary Literature at Yale University, where he taught for forty years before retiring in 1998. In addition to hundreds of critical articles, his work, which focuses on Holocaust and Judaic Studies, includes *A Critics Journey: Literary Reflections, 1958–1998* (1999), *The Longest Shadow* (2002), and *Scars of the Spirit* (2002).

A descendent of William Wordsworth's brother Christopher, JONATHAN WORDSWORTH is Professor Emeritus of English Literature at Oxford and President of The Wordsworth Trust. Jonathan Wordsworth has published several definitive editions of the poet's work, including facsimile editions with the Woodstock Facsimile series, *Revolution and Romanticism*. Recent books include *The Prelude: The Four Texts* (1996), *The Bright Work Grows* (1997), and *The New Penguin Book of Romantic Poetry* (2002) with Jessica Wordsworth.

INDEX